Forthcoming Volumes in the New
Church's Teaching Series

The Anglican Vision
James E. Griffiss

Opening the Bible
Roger Ferlo

Engaging the Word
Michael Johnston

The Practice of Prayer
Margaret Guenther

Living with History
Fredrica Harris Thompsett

Early Christian Traditions
Rebecca Lyman

Opening the Prayer Book
Jeffrey D. Lee

Mysteries of Faith
Mark McIntosh

The Christian Social Witness
Harold Lewis

Liturgical Prayer
Louis Weil

Ethics After Easter
Stephen Holmgren

Christian Wholeness
Martin L. Smith, SSJE

The Anglican Vision

The New
Church's Teaching Series
Volume 1

The
Anglican
Vision

James E. Griffiss

COWLEY PUBLICATIONS
Cambridge ✦ Boston
Massachusetts

The title *The Church's Teaching Series* is used by permission of the Domestic and Foreign Missionary Society. Use of the series title does not constitute the Society's endorsement of the content of the work.

Library of Congress Cataloging in Publication Data:
Griffiss, James E., 1928–
    The Anglican vision / James E. Griffiss.
        p.   cm.   — (The new church's teaching series ; v. 1)
    Includes bibliographical references.
    ISBN 1-56101-143-6 (alk. paper)
    1. Episcopal Church. 2. Anglican Communion—United States.
    3. Anglican communion. I. Title. II. Series.
    BX5930.2.G74   1997
    283'.73—dc21   97-21731
                                                                        CIP

Scripture quotations are from the *New Revised Standard Version* of the Bible, © 1989 by the Division of Christian Education of the National Council of the Churches of Christ in the USA. Used by permission. All rights reserved.

Editor: Cynthia Shattuck; Copyeditor and Designer: Vicki Black
Study Guide by Cynthia Shattuck and Vicki Black
Cover art from *Windows* (oil on canvas, 1912) by Robert Delaunay

Royalties from the sale of books in the New Church's Teaching Series have been donated to the *Anglican Theological Review*.

This book is printed on recycled, acid-free paper and was produced in Canada.

Second Printing

Cowley Publications
28 Temple Place • *Boston, Massachusetts 02111*
1-800-225-1534 • *http://www.cowley.org/~cowley*

Contents

The New Church's Teaching Series

Almost fifty years ago a series for the Episcopal Church called The Church's Teaching was launched with the publication of Robert Dentan's *The Holy Scriptures* in 1949, and again in the 1970s the church commissioned another teaching series for the next generation of Anglicans. Originally the series was part of an effort to give the growing postwar churches a sense of Anglican identity: what Anglicans share with the larger Christian community and what makes them distinctive within it. During that seemingly more tranquil era it may have been easier to reach a consensus and to speak authoritatively. Now, at the end of the twentieth century, consensus and authority are more difficult; there is considerably more diversity of belief and practice within the churches today, and more people than ever who have never been introduced to the church at all.

The books in this new teaching series for the Episcopal Church attempt to encourage and respond to the times—and to the challenges that will usher out the old century and bring in the new. This new series differs from the previous two in significant ways: it has no official status, claims no special authority, speaks in a personal voice, and comes not out of committees but from scholars and pastors meeting and talking informally together. It assumes a different readership: adults who are not "cradle Anglicans," but who come from other religious traditions or from no tradition at all, and who want to know what Anglicanism has to offer.

As the series editor I want to thank E. Allen Kelley, former president of Morehouse Publishing, for initially inviting me to bring together a group of teachers and pastors who could write with learning and conviction about their faith. I am grateful both to him and to Morehouse for participating in the early development of the series.

Since those initial conversations there have been substantial changes in the series itself, but its basic purpose has remained: to explore the themes of the Christian life through Holy Scripture, historical and contemporary theology, worship, spirituality, and social witness. It is our hope that all readers, Anglicans and otherwise, will find the books an aid in their continuing growth into Christ.

James E. Griffiss
Series Editor

Acknowledgments

I want to express my appreciation to Cynthia Shattuck and Vicki Black of Cowley Publications for their extensive reworking of my original manuscript. They encouraged and helped me to develop it as a book appropriate for study groups by rearranging the material and clarifying many of my ideas. I am also grateful to Gardiner Shattuck for reading various chapters as they developed; his knowledge of the history of the Episcopal Church has been invaluable. Of course, any limitations the book may have are my responsibility.

I also want to express my gratitude to the other authors in this series who through conversations and criticisms contributed to the development of this book.

Finally, I have written this book in thanksgiving for the ministry of Daniel Corrigan, Bishop in the Church of God, who through his life of witness taught me much about belief in the God of Jesus Christ.

PART I

The Origins of Anglicanism

Chapter 1

From England
to Portage

O ne of the great bishops of the Episcopal Church, Daniel
Corrigan, liked to tell a story about his early days as
a newly ordained deacon. He was sent by his bishop to
Portage, a small town in Wisconsin, to build up a mission
congregation. When he arrived in the town on a Saturday
to begin his work, he asked one of the local people where
the Episcopal church was. The man responded, "The Episcopal church—what's that? Never heard of it." The young
deacon, still full of all he had learned in seminary, proceeded
to tell the man that the Episcopal Church was part of the
worldwide Anglican Church, in communion with the
Church of England and the Archbishop of Canterbury. The
man replied, "England! Then what you doin' here in Portage?"

In all probability the early Christian missionaries in
pagan Rome were asked a similar question: "Jesus of
Nazareth! A Jew! What's he got to do with Rome?" And, so
we are told in the book of Acts, much the same thing
happened to Paul when he preached in Athens: "He seems
to be a proclaimer of foreign divinities," the sophisticated
Athenians said of him (Acts 17:18).

These questions about the significance of the church and its message are still valid today. At least Paul and the other early Christian missionaries could preach a new savior, Jesus the Christ, to the people of Rome or Athens. What they had to say was not only new but startling. Their gospel offered hope in a weary world, the forgiveness of sins, and resurrection from the dead, and it sought to replace the many divinities of Greece and Rome with one God, with one Lord and Savior who had been born and who died and was raised from the dead. The young deacon in Portage, however, faced a situation which in some ways was much more difficult. Jesus Christ from Nazareth was already being preached in Portage by Lutherans, Roman Catholics, and Methodists. The message about him was neither new nor startling; it had been spoken and heard many times before. Who was this deacon with his talk about England? What did he have to offer that was new and saving to people who had heard it all before and who, to make matters even worse, were of good Nordic and Germanic stock and who had even less respect for the English than the Athenians and Romans had for the Jews?

First it needs to be said that we Anglicans, like Paul and the other early Christian missionaries, have only one thing to offer: the gospel—the Good News—of Jesus Christ. To paraphrase St. Paul: We preach Christ crucified, whom God raised from the dead for us and for our salvation (1 Cor. 1:23). Without that Good News the church has no reason for existence, except, perhaps, to be another social service agency devoted to good works or another club of like-minded people. So, as the young deacon eventually learned—and this was the point of his story—he had been sent to Portage to preach the gospel, not to talk about the Archbishop of Canterbury or the Anglican Communion.

Nonetheless, Roman Catholics, Methodists, and Lutherans in Portage were also preaching the gospel of Jesus Christ, so why was an Anglican version of the gospel needed? What did the Episcopal Church have to offer that was different from the gospel preached by the other churches? Of course, there were many people in Portage who needed to hear the gospel for the first time—people who were not Roman Catholics, Lutherans, Methodists, or anything else—so there was ample opportunity for the young deacon. But, as Bishop Corrigan liked to say later in his life when he was telling this story, the question of "What you doin' here in Portage?" always haunted him.

It is a question which still needs an answer from those of us who call ourselves Episcopalians, whether we are in Portage, Wisconsin, or in any other place in which the Episcopal Church is found or to which it may go. What are we doing here? Do we have something of importance to say which gives us a mission to the vast number of people who have heard of Jesus Christ, but for whom the story of his life, death, and resurrection has never become Good News? Do we have anything more to say to people for whom belief in Jesus Christ is deep and central to their lives, but who have become alienated from the Christian community out of anger or rejection, or who simply have questions and problems their own churches are unwilling to confront?

Despite the response of the man from Portage, the Episcopal Church is, in fact, a well-established institution in America. Many people look at it as just another church—fine for those who like that kind of thing, but certainly not for everyone. In the recent past the popular perception of the Episcopal Church was that of a church appealing mainly to the rich and socially prominent, whose membership in the Episcopal Church helped them on their upward path. When I was growing up in Baltimore during the 1930s and 1940s, the Episcopal churches (along with the Presbyterian) were the place for the fashionable weddings and funerals that were reported prominently on the society page in the local newspaper. Episcopalians, in spite of their small numbers, were powerful figures in city politics and finances, usually working out of sight to maintain the status quo in the city. They were portrayed in films like *The Bishop's Wife* or *Father Knows Best* as very proper, somewhat aristocratic, and Episcopal clergy often had a slightly British accent that passed for being "upper class." Some vestiges of that past are still with us, but the Episcopal Church is no longer perceived as the church of the rich and powerful.

If the banker J. P. Morgan and many influential industrialists were Episcopalians, so were lesser-known social reformers at the turn of the century like Vida Scudder and Frederick Huntington, people who identified the Episcopal Church with organized labor or with immigrants in the slums of eastern cities. Many Episcopal clergy were active during the Civil Rights movement of the 1950s and 1960s; one of the Episcopalians marching for racial integration, a young seminarian named Jonathan Daniels, was killed in Selma. In the following decade, the decision of the Episcopal Church in 1976 to ordain women to the priesthood and the episcopate was a prophetic action for a church that had often been considered stuffy and hidebound by tradition.

Today the Episcopal Church is a church whose members continue that tradition of advocating for unpopular political and social causes: ministry to those with AIDS, for example, or opposition to war and all forms of injustice. Like other churches, we are struggling to discern God's will in the complex questions of human sexuality. So the Episcopal Church these days is not a launching place for the powerful or a calm and peaceful harbor for those seeking refuge from a turbulent world. It is, rather, a church in which issues are ardently debated and crises faced, however reluctantly at times; and, most important of all, it is a church in which people pray for guidance and the presence of the Holy Spirit in understanding and resolving those issues.

In other words, there is much more to the Episcopal Church than meets the eye of the casual observer who sees only the quaint church on the corner. In spite of its eccentricities and peculiarities, in spite of its stereotyped image, and even in spite of its sins and failures, the Episcopal Church is first and foremost a *church:* it is a gathering of committed people who believe in and attempt to proclaim and live out daily the Good News of Jesus Christ. It is a community in which many people with all sorts of backgrounds, interests, strengths, and weaknesses find the grace and power of God through worship, prayer, community life, and outreach to others.

The Episcopal Church is also part of a community of Christians in Africa, Asia, Latin America, Europe, North America, and elsewhere in the world whose practices, hopes, and customs can be quite different from those of Americans, yet who are united by a common belief in Jesus Christ as Savior and Lord. The Anglican Communion, as it is called, now numbers far more people of color than of British or European origin, and English is no longer its only language. Though we are not always cognizant of our broader identity, we in the Episcopal Church form only a small part of a much larger communion of churches.

～

If the Episcopal Church is not what its stereotype might indicate, then what is it? What do we who are Episcopalians have to say about Jesus Christ in a way that is distinctive? What do we have to say that changes the lives of the people in Portage, Wisconsin or anywhere else? One way of answering these questions is to look at the origins of the Episcopal Church and of Anglicanism itself—how it came into being, what it has believed and what it continues to believe, how it has grown and developed through the centuries. Before we turn to that story, however, I want to relate a more personal history of what it has meant for me to hear the gospel of Jesus Christ in this particular community of faith over the past fifty years.

The story of my experience with the Episcopal Church spans a period of tremendous and often threatening cultural and social change for people like me, when the foundations of much that I once believed about myself and God have been not only shaken but in some cases destroyed. The securities of family and position in my white, Anglo-Saxon, middle-class world are no longer guaranteed. Our images of God have become more inclusive: God is no longer the exclusive property of the middle class. In the midst of such foundational changes many people today wonder what the church, whether Episcopal or any other, has to do with their lives. Perhaps this story of my years in the Episcopal Church will give some insight into how I have answered that question for myself.

I was confirmed in the Episcopal Church about fifty years ago. I came to it from the kind of mixed background that is not uncommon in the religious stew of the United States: my mother was an active Methodist and my father a lapsed Episcopalian. My mother regularly took me as a child to her Methodist church on Sundays, and relatives of my father would occasionally take me to the Episcopal church on special occasions. Shortly after I was confirmed, my father's great aunt said to me that she was so glad I had "returned home"—my father's family had been Episcopalians for many generations. I think that now, with the hindsight of years, I would prefer to say that I "found a home." The Episcopal Church became for me a saving community, that is, one in which I have received the grace to hear the Good News and even, with all my failures and sins, to have my life shaped by the gospel of Jesus Christ.

The security I knew after World War II—that is, the late 1940s, the time when I came of age—derived from a society which was centered in the church and a political order which was reasonably stable. It was a time of religious revival, as so often happens after a major war. Churches of every denomination were full and money for programs was abundant; students in colleges and universities turned to the Christian churches for direction and meaning in their lives, and there was considerable academic and intellectual interest in religious matters. T. S. Eliot and W. H. Auden, for example, were for many people living examples of the harmony of religion with the arts and the intellectual life. That both were Anglicans was, of course, even better for those of us who were Episcopalians. It was a time when it was intellectually and socially "respectable" to be religious, although the religion which we knew was still fairly traditional.

Mainstream religion as I remember it tended to be nostalgic; it looked back to a time when the United States could still be thought of as a Christian nation in which the church shaped the political and cultural life of the people. Indeed, for some of my generation religion was a hearkening back to the Middle Ages when Christian philosophy and arts flourished. A revival of interest in medieval philosophy and theology appeared in some academic circles, for example, led by the neo-scholastic philosopher J. Maritain and the historian E. Gilson, and late medieval writers like Dante were popular. The moral, spiritual, political, and social values with which my generation grew up were still fairly clear; on the surface, at least, they were the norms that governed our lives. There were certain things we did not do, and what we did do was determined by those who set the norms: parents, clergy, teachers, and all who had power and authority. We also believed that the American dream would be realized and that God was in the heavens and all was right with the world and ourselves—despite the occasional setback or misstep. We knew our place in that world, and those who were racially, economically, or sexually different knew theirs, and stayed there. After the war the United States had become the most powerful nation in the world, and we Americans had a strong sense of our superiority and moral rightness.

At least that was the perception. Other forces were at work underneath that surface security. Human beings were no less confused and frightened then than they have been at any other time in history, though we may have been better at hiding it and better at pretending that all was well. As we witnessed the rise of Communism and the start of the Cold War, those of us who were restless or troubled, and felt ourselves to be outsiders in many ways to the comfortable world of our parents, knew not to ask too many questions about the prevailing political and economic policies of this country.

Yet it was also a time when some of these dominant values began, very tentatively, to be called into question. The war had changed the attitude of many people toward sex, for example, especially those who had served in the armed forces. They had come into contact with other cultures where norms were less restrictive than those of most middle-class Americans, and their more relaxed attitude about sexual relations between women and men and even about homosexuality slowly began to spread. My generation began to be affected as well by new literary movements; we read James Joyce, Marcel Proust, Henry Miller, and Ezra Pound. We went to small movie theaters to watch what we called "art films," especially those from France, which talked about sex far more explicitly than the Hollywood movies with which we had grown up. While most of us still conformed to the traditional norms in public, there was certainly a sense that things were changing in private.

All these things had much to do with how my generation understood the church. In such an increasingly changing world, as it seemed to be, God and God's church were a source of comfort and an assurance that all was well. We looked upon the church as a bulwark against the dangers to our world and, at the same time, a strong force for what we believed to be morality and the spiritual improvement of society.

In such a society it was very easy to confuse the norms of our white, middle-class culture with Christianity. In my home parish it was simply assumed, for example, that young men and women would eventually settle down, get married, raise a family, and live a comfortable and prosperous life in the suburbs, safely away from the more threatening cities—such was the Christian way of things. The world of business and politics was still in the hands of men; women stayed at home and took care of the household. People from what we now call "minority groups" were kept in their "place," a place which was largely menial and politically and economically powerless. We understood Christian faith and practice, in other words, in terms of the values which society held up to us.

The church which I knew in Maryland during the 1940s, in spite of the rumbling noises underneath, was a bastion of social and political conformity. To a considerable degree it supported the status quo as the way God had ordained matters. In most parish churches the biblical words of judgment about conformity to social mores spoken by the prophets of the Hebrew scriptures and by Jesus himself were either not heard or were interpreted away. Very rarely were sermons preached about racial and economic justice; that all churches in Baltimore were racially segregated never caused most Christians any problem whatsoever. The church was simply a part of what we later learned to call The Establishment.

I was certainly no youthful prophet, and I was quite willing to conform to most of the rules which governed my life; but even I began to sense that all was not right with the economic and racial policies of our society and of the church which supported that society. I began to see that something was missing in a church which itself maintained policies of racial segregation, for example, or invested in slum housing, or was not willing to deal realistically with changing values about sexuality.

It was not really until the 1950s that things began to change. Prophetic political leaders challenged the status quo, standing against the Communist witch hunts carried on by Joseph McCarthy in the U. S. Senate and, like Eleanor Roosevelt, advocating for racial justice. Prophets within the church called us to hear and pay attention to what the gospel of Jesus Christ had to say about conformity to the world and its values. James Pike, when he was dean of the Cathedral of St. John the Divine in New York, preached passionately against segregation in church institutions and organizations. Groups like the Episcopal Society for Racial and Cultural Unity began to recall the Episcopal Church to its nineteenth-century heritage of the social gospel movement and the Depression years, when Episcopalians worked for economic justice—a heritage which had been forgotten.[1] These prophetic voices began to provide a fresh hearing of the gospel.

At that time I was studying at The General Theological Seminary in New York City. There I heard of Paul Moore, later to be Bishop of New York, and Kilmer Meyers, who became Bishop of California, along with several others working in a depressed urban area of New Jersey. Trinity Parish in New York City began to use its considerable financial resources to support work on the lower East Side of the city, an area of tremendous poverty. A group of us in seminary were so inspired that we began a mission to the vagrants and homeless who surrounded the neighborhood of the seminary. We also began to provide breakfast and religious instruction once a week to the Puertorican school children in the area and to become involved with what was then a large immigrant population in New York.

Neither of those ventures was very successful at the time, but they did help a new generation of clergy to hear the gospel in a new way and to question many of our inherited assumptions about God, Christ, the Bible, and the calling of the Episcopal Church. I have always remembered, for example, a young, street-wise girl in one of my released time classes. I was talking about how Jesus had died for our sins and what a difference that should make in our lives. It was a typical young seminarian's sermon—pompous and quite unrelated to the realities of life in the city as she knew it. The young girl looked at me and said simply,

"Who asked him to?" It was a question that still haunts me whenever I preach or teach.

In the churches of the 1950s there were also new theological stirrings after World War II, when scholars in Europe and the United States could once again communicate with one another. At mid-century Episcopalians were studying the work of continental Protestant theologians. By then Paul Tillich was teaching in New York, and the work of other theologians like Rudolf Bultmann, Emil Brunner, Karl Barth, and Dietrich Bonhoeffer began to stir the quiet waters of all churches in the United States. Karl Barth taught a more radical theology of the cross and redemption than we Episcopalians had ever heard, and Paul Tillich made us pay attention to cultural shifts and changes. Teachers like Norman Pittenger, with whom I studied at The General Seminary, began to address new theological movements—the authority of the Bible in a more complex world, how to understand the nature of God in a culture increasingly dominated by science, and the relation of Christianity to other religious traditions.

Those of us in the rich parts of the world had to face up to the end of colonialism in Africa and Asia, wondering what that might mean for Christians like us, who identified Christian faith with European and American culture. We began to hear about racial policies in South Africa from the Anglican priest Trevor Huddlestone, who struggled for a Christian witness against apartheid. In the 1950s not much was yet being said about leadership roles of women in the church—Elizabeth Dyer had been elected to the House of Deputies in 1946 but the General Convention deputies had quickly voted to exclude women in the future—and sexuality was still talked about only in whispers. But for those who were willing to listen, quiet voices advocating change could be heard.

I had been fortunate in that the parish church to which I belonged in downtown Baltimore, which at one time had been fashionable and wealthy, reflected some of these concerns. During World War II the neighborhood had changed dramatically, and many of the old townhouses had become rooming houses for an itinerant population. The clergy had to balance a ministry between the relatively affluent who were still left and the new neighbors. As a result the congregation was mixed economically and socially. That church was the first place in which I began to realize that not everyone in the Episcopal Church shared the social and family values which I had known, that morality had to do with social justice as well as sex, and that ultimately "sin" had more to do with failure to love God and my neighbor than with following rules. I had had the good experience of learning that the church could be a place where those who were questioning and even rebelling were welcomed and where wounds could be healed and *real* sins acknowledged, confessed, and forgiven. Consequently, when changes began to occur in the Episcopal Church while I was in seminary, I was ready—with what was, I now realize, a certain amount of brashness and self righteousness—to jump into the battles that were beginning.

Ordained in 1954, I became the young assistant in a large, conservative, and wealthy parish in Baltimore and did the usual thing for my generation and age: I joined liberal political action groups and organized protests against the racial policies of the diocese, which still maintained a racially segregated summer camp for children. The younger people in the parish thought me an ally against the more established and older members of the congregation, who still, they believed, did not understand that the world had changed. I organized a group of young married women, for example, who had children to care for in the daytime and so had to meet in the evenings to talk. The older women, who had grown up with servants, met during the daytime in an organization called the Woman's Auxiliary and found it difficult to accept the existence of another women's group.

During those two years as curate I found that trying to teach and preach the new liturgical, biblical, and theological ideas I had learned in seminary was really what excited me most, and so I went off to graduate school, studied philosophy, received a Ph.D. in 1961, and began teaching. My first job was in a new seminary of the Episcopal Church in Puerto Rico established with the hope of expanding the work of the church in Latin America by educating for the ordained ministry people from the Caribbean and Central America—a bold experiment in mission at the time. During the ten years I spent there, the theological ideas that had begun to develop in seminary, parish ministry, and graduate school about what it meant to be a Christian in a time of radical change started to come together. But also in that church environment, so different from any I had known before, I began to learn much more about what it meant to be an Anglican.

Because the students were so varied—-from Haiti, the former British West Indies, and the Spanish-speaking countries of Central America—they forced me to ask what it was in Anglicanism that appealed to them. Before, I had simply assumed that all Anglicans came from a background fundamentally similar to my own: English-speakers living in a reasonably free and prosperous society. It had never occurred to me that being an Episcopalian might require any great sacrifice of language or culture, but here were people who became Anglicans at great personal cost. For them Anglicanism and the Episcopal Church represented a foreign culture, or, for those from the British West Indies, a colonial power. What was it that attracted them to such a church?

During those ten years I gradually learned. What they found in Anglicanism, despite all the cultural differences, was a way of believing, worshiping, and living that was grounded in the heritage of early Christianity but which was also open to working with all the changes and developments taking place in their world. In other words, they valued a church which tried to live with *both* tradition *and* change. Many of the students saw in Anglicanism a community in which the tradition of Christian faith could become a powerful force for liberation in the present.

I also had to learn to pray in other languages, with different images and metaphors for God, and to talk about God and other human beings with different concepts. Not all of my students had been educated in the philosophical and theological tradition of the United States and Europe, as I had been, and so I had to find ways of communicating the Christian faith that drew upon religious and cultural assumptions quite different from my own. These assumptions were derived from African and Indian religious traditions such as Voodoo and the syncretism of Catholicism and the older Indian religions that had flourished in the region before the Spanish, British, and American missionaries had arrived.

These experiences of other cultures helped prepare me for my return in 1971 to the United States and to a culture that appeared to be radically different from the one I had left before going to Puerto Rico. Many historians now think that the apparently stable world of the 1950s and early 1960s in America was itself an aberration, and that the late 1960s and 1970s represented a return to the more fluid society of an earlier time. From my vantage point as a professor of theology at Nashotah House, a conservative and somewhat isolated Episcopal seminary in the upper midwest, I watched and took part in the changes in the Episcopal Church as women were ordained to the priesthood and episcopate, and the 1928 Prayer Book, which had nourished several generations of Episcopalians, gave way to the 1979 *Book of Common Prayer*, and questions about sexuality began to be aired.

Today the Episcopal Church still continues to debate questions surrounding ordination and sexuality. Episcopalians still struggle to create more just policies on racial and gender relations, economic inequality, and political involvement. The Episcopal Church is no longer controlled exclusively by one economic and social group; it is rapidly becoming truly multicultural and more representative of American society. It is also pursuing serious ecumenical conversations with other Christian bodies, especially the Evangelical Lutheran Church in America.

In other words, a church that values the past and the tradition of Christian belief and practice is increasingly willing to deal with the present and future, and to come to terms with the conditions of American political and cultural life under which Christians actually live. It has struggled to hear God's word to us through the tradition *and* in the new conditions facing Christian people.

In many ways I am a conservative person, and I miss some of the comforts and securities of the Episcopal Church I once knew. Like the Israelites of old, I do not always find it easy to give up the cucumbers of life in Egypt for the manna of the desert of Sinai, even though I know that the securities of the past were paid for by slavery and that the desert is on the way to the Promised Land. After the Israelites arrived in the Promised Land they still grumbled and complained, and I suspect that I, and some other Episcopalians, shall also. We all do have to remember, however, that it was on Mount Sinai, *in the desert*, that God gave the Israelites a new and astounding knowledge of the divine will and purpose for human life.

Can we who have conformed to the political institutions and cultural values of a world that is rapidly changing into something quite new understand how to proclaim and witness to our faith in Jesus Christ in this emerging society? Can those who never knew that world, because they are too young, value the past and its authentic traditions? How do we maintain continuity with the tradition of belief that we have received, and yet also adapt and change according to the times?

It is my belief that in the Christian faith as the Episcopal Church has received it there are abundant resources for meeting these challenges of the future. In the chapters that follow I hope to identify some of the resources of our past that will enable us as a church to face the new questions of the future honestly, while being firmly grounded in the source of our faith: that God is in Christ, reconciling the world.

Chapter 2

The Beginnings
of Anglicanism

When the man in Portage, Wisconsin, asked what the Episcopal Church was, he certainly did not have in mind a lecture on its historical origins and why it was part of the Anglican Communion. In all probability he simply meant he didn't know where the building was. Yet many who have found our way to the Episcopal Church do want to know what distinguishes it from all the other churches in town. What does the Episcopal Church stand for? Why is it here? Where did it come from?

My purpose in this chapter is to tell something of the early history of Anglicanism and even to try to explain how the Episcopal Church got to Portage. In speaking of Anglicanism's origins, however, I want to focus less on the details of its history and more on those larger themes of tradition, continuity, and change that help us to define what Anglicanism is. There are several excellent histories already available; my task here is to interpret those themes in the light of our history and to concentrate on those figures and movements that have informed our understanding of Anglicanism.

Since the Episcopal Church in the United States had its origin in the Church of England, we must first look at its roots in England at the time of the Reformation. The Reformation was a period of great upheaval in Europe, politically and culturally as well as theologically. Politically, the last remnants of the Holy Roman Empire, that loose federation of Christian and Roman Catholic rulers who claimed to be a continuation of the old Roman Empire, were breaking up. By the time of the Reformation the unity of the federation was more in name than reality and the religious and political unity was increasingly giving way to emerging nation states. Kings and princes in Germany, England, and France, chiefly, were asserting their independence and establishing their own authority before Martin Luther posted his ninety-five theses on the church door in Wittenberg.

Culturally, the Reformation period followed upon the Renaissance and the new ideas emerging from the rediscovery of the classical learning of Greece and Rome and the beginning of scientific and historical investigation. A growing sense of individualism was encouraged by the breakdown of the medieval ideal of a Christian commonwealth established by God through the Catholic Church, and an emerging middle class gained more power in political and religious affairs.

These political and cultural movements informed the theological battles that took place during the Reformation. The breakup of the Catholic Church, centered in Rome and the papacy, was not just the result of a theological quarrel; it was a sociological development as well. The theological differences between the reformers and the Roman Catholic Church were linked to radical changes politically and culturally as new centers of power emerged on the continent.

Some of the princes in the German states sided with Luther for political reasons as much as for theological ones.

Moreover, when the theological issues came to the fore, both Martin Luther and John Calvin, the primary leaders of the Reformation in Europe, did not think of themselves as beginning *new* churches. Both appealed beyond the pope to the primitive church of Holy Scripture and the early councils, and claimed that their reforms were simply returning the church to a past uncorrupted by later doctrinal accretions. All the while, however, they put forward what was in fact a new understanding of that past, for they interpreted the relationship of Christians to God in the light of their theological convictions about faith and authority in the church.

The changes that took place in the Church of England at the time of the Reformation reflected the same tension present in the continental churches: a claim of continuity with the past, even while making changes in response to a new theological, political, and cultural situation. That tension has continued to characterize the Anglicanism that emerged from the Reformation controversies, so it is important to see something of its origins at the beginning of our history.

The initial demand for change in the Church of England was quite straightforward. The Church of England broke with the authority of the pope in Rome, and what the papacy represented as the center of Catholic tradition, for very practical and political reasons: King Henry VIII wanted an annulment of his marriage so that he could marry again and thus hope to obtain a male heir to the throne. His failure to procure an annulment and his subsequent break with Rome opened up other demands as well—landowners, especially among the rising middle class, desired control of church property; radical elements in the church sought more religious freedom; and certain intellectuals in the universities wanted to put into practice the biblical and theological insights of the continental reformers.

But in spite of the radical changes these demands represented, virtually everyone in power, both in the church and in the state, professed that the reformed Church of England, far from departing from Catholic tradition, was simply returning to the pure doctrine and practice of the ancient Catholic Church, the church of the apostolic fathers, before Rome had gained power and authority. It is doubtful that any save the most extreme thought of themselves as starting a *new* church. Nor did they think of themselves as enunciating profound theological principles about continuity and change—although this is in fact what they did. They simply wanted to purify and reform the tradition.

Of course, much confusion followed the changes that began under Henry VIII. Those who remained faithful to Rome resisted the changes and those who looked to the reformers on the continent demanded even greater reforms. It was not until the reign of Queen Elizabeth I that the Church of England began to settle down and develop a theological understanding of what had been going on. But even after the Elizabethan Settlement of the national church, confusion continued through the reigns of the Stuarts, the Commonwealth (when the Puritans gained control of church and state), and the eventual restoration of the monarchy and the reestablishment of the Church of England under Charles II.

Looking back upon this period of confusion in the English church, it is quite clear that the Church of England did change in crucial ways—ways that have defined Angli-can churches ever since. First and most radical of all, the authority of the pope to teach and define Christian belief was repudiated. In its place a new authority was given to the Bible. Like the reformers on the continent, the leaders of the Church of England turned to scripture as the primary source for authority in matters of belief and practice, asserting that beliefs and practices which could not be justified in scripture could not be required of Christians. Thus many teachings and customs of the Roman church were rejected—celibacy for the clergy, masses for the dead, indulgences, and the invocation of the saints, for example. There was also a new emphasis upon preaching. In agree-ment with the teachings of both Calvin and Luther, the English reformers believed that preaching the word of God as found in the Bible led to repentance and faith. The Bible was therefore translated into English so that it could be read by all, and was read publicly in the church services.

Politically too, there were significant changes. The Crown—the monarch and Parliament—assumed authority for the governance of the church, so that lay people began to have more control over church affairs. Bishops were appointed by the Crown, rather than by the pope, and landowners controlled appointments to many parish churches. The pope was declared to be only another "for-eign prince" without political or ecclesiastical authority in England.

On the other hand, the established church, as it became under Elizabeth, unlike some of the reformed churches on the continent, retained the substance of the older traditions of belief and practice in many respects. Most notably was the threefold ministry of bishops, priests, and deacons, and the claim that bishops continued in historic succession from the earliest apostles. In the *Book of Common Prayer* baptism and the Holy Eucharist remained central, and the prayer book clearly envisioned a sacramental pattern of Christian worship along with an ordered structure of public prayer in the offices of Morning and Evening Prayer. The ancient creeds—the Apostles' Creed, the Nicene Creed, and the Athanasian Creed—remained the foundation of the church's teaching about the essential doctrines of Christian faith: the Trinity, the Incarnation, and the presence of the Holy Spirit in the church and in the life of individuals. The Church of England continued to be regarded as the ancient Catholic Church of the nation, tracing its origins back to the sixth-century Augustine of Canterbury. It was the church that by law, if not always in practice, incorporated all the people of England into one worshiping and believing community.

Part of the process of bringing order out of the confusion of the reformation of the Church of England was the production of the Articles of Religion (commonly known as the Thirty-Nine Articles) in 1571, during the reign of Queen Elizabeth. The Articles set forth both basic Christian doctrine as held by the Church of England (the doctrines of the Trinity, the Incarnation, the work of the Holy Spirit) and also those teachings that were highly controversial—the authority of the church and the ministry, justification, the importance of good works, and predestination. They also condemned certain "Romish" teachings and practices that were regarded as superstitious. The Articles were quite obviously eclectic, unlike the confessions produced by the reformed churches on the continent. They were intended to make room for different theological views within a national church in a time of great division and disagreement.[1]

It was not until the seventeenth century that theologians of the Church of England began to develop a theological rationale for the changes; as is so often the case, theological reflection followed upon historical events. In the wake of so much upheaval and change, the Church of England felt it had much to justify. On the one hand it had to satisfy itself that it had not abandoned the Catholic faith and tradition, as Roman Catholics charged; on the other hand, that it also had gone as far as it could in terms of theological and ecclesiastical reform in order to satisfy its more extreme Calvinist wing. As the Puritans began to emerge as a powerful group in the Church of England, with their distrust of clerical hierarchy and insistence on the sole authority of the Bible, interpreted by conscience, Anglicans also had to justify holding onto their older traditions of belief and practice.

The theologian who responded most successfully to all the opponents of the Church of England was Richard Hooker, writing his *Laws of Ecclesiastical Polity* at the end of the sixteenth century. His method of dealing with theological questions has remained characteristic of much Anglican theology ever since—maintaining continuity with the tradition the church has received from the past while seeking to accommodate the changes new situations require. The central purpose of his work was defending the social and ecclesiastical status quo in England, which was threatened by the independence and individualism of the English Roman Catholics and the Puritans. Therefore he justified Anglicanism as a way between the extremities of radical Protestantism and Roman Catholicism—the *via media*, as it later came to be called. Hooker argued that the strength of Anglicanism lay in its search for mediation between the conflicting claims of infallibility, whether of the Bible or of the pope. He sought a balance that would be more than simple compromise or expediency—a way of moving forward between those claims and differences. For

Hooker this way of mediation rested upon the assurance of our faith in the incarnation of God in Christ combined with a willingness to accept the limitations of our knowledge in secondary matters. Thus, on the one hand he rejected the claims of Rome to make dogmatic assertions that did not derive from scripture; on the other hand he rejected the extreme Protestant claim that the only source of Christian belief about God and the practice of the church is to be found in the Bible.

Hooker certainly shared with the Protestant reformers the belief that scripture was the "oracle of God" and that it contained all that was necessary for salvation. Scripture is the witness to the central faith of Christians in Jesus Christ; it makes known to us the Good News of God's saving work. Yet Hooker also allowed that scripture must be interpreted in the light of human understanding and experience (what he called reason) and in the context of the church as the continuing tradition of worship and belief. The Bible does not stand alone. Thus he distinguished between what is fundamental in the Bible, namely, the way of salvation in Christ, from what is secondary, a human recounting of events that must always be interpreted by the church in the light of Christ. Our relationship to God, Hooker argued, is multifaceted, and no one way can exclude all others. The Bible is a fundamental source of our knowledge of God, but we also learn about God through human experience and rational reflection—the balance of scripture, tradition, and reason, which Anglicans traditionally refer to as "the three-legged stool."

Of Hooker's approach to the authority of scripture, tradition, and reason, Archbishop Michael Ramsey wrote,

> [Hooker's] theology claimed to do both far less and far more than the theologies of Calvin, of Luther, and of

Trent. It did less in that it eschewed any attempt to offer a complete scheme of biblical doctrine, or an experiential assurance of justification, or an infallibilist system of dogma. It did more in that it appealed to a larger field of authority and dealt with the whole person...both by its reverence for reason and conscience and by its refusal to draw a circle around the inward personal element in religion and to separate it from the world of external things....The claim of this theology to be "Catholic" rested not only upon its affinity with antiquity but upon the true "wholeness" of its authorities and of its treatment of human beings and their need. It offered them not only justification in their inward self but the sanctification of their whole being through sharing in the divine life.[2]

In the last sentence Michael Ramsey points also to the third dimension of Hooker's theology, one which has become vital to contemporary Anglican spirituality, most clearly in the 1979 *Book of Common Prayer:* our participation or sharing in the divine life through the sacramental life of the church. Hooker was a strong sacramentalist. The fifth book of his *Laws* is largely concerned with the relationship of the two sacraments of baptism and eucharist to the Incarnation. There he argues that through the union of God with our humanity in the Incarnation we human beings are called into the life of God. We know our calling and the means through which we are able to fulfill that calling in the sacraments of baptism and eucharist. Those two fundamental sacramental actions are the means of grace through which we grow into God and become the sons and daughters of God through Christ.

We will continue to see how these three themes of Hooker's *Laws*—Anglicanism as a middle way, the authority of scripture, tradition, and reason, and our sacramental sharing in the divine life—work out in Anglican history, becoming, as shall see, more fully developed in the nineteenth century and in our own time.

At the same time that these developments were taking place within the Church of England, Anglicanism and its controversies were brought by British settlers to the American colonies. Prior to American independence it was not possible to speak of "the Episcopal Church," since Anglicanism in the colonies was primarily an extension of the Church of England. Its ministers came from or went to England to be ordained, while its churches were assisted financially by missionary groups such as the Society for the Propagation of the Gospel in Foreign Parts. Proponents of Anglicanism hoped that through the missionary efforts of the SPG it would come to replace other forms of religious expression—chiefly Puritanism and Quakerism—but the religion of the American colonies continued to remain pluralistic.

In the south Anglicanism was the church of the privileged, particularly in Virginia and South Carolina, whereas in the middle colonies of New Jersey, Delaware, Maryland, and Pennsylvania, Anglicanism was one religious choice among many. In New England, which was settled by the Puritans and their descendants, Anglicanism lacked power and influence but was spiritually far more vital than in the colonies where it was the established religion. At the beginning of the Revolution the Church of England was the second largest denomination in America, after Congregationalism, with over four hundred congregations.[3]

Throughout the eighteenth century most Anglicans in England and America were moderate Deists, which was not surprising given the prevailing intellectual and political outlook. Many of the principles enshrined in the Declaration of Independence and the Bill of Rights derived from Enlightenment and Deist ideas. The effect of Deism upon the religious life of the Episcopal Church in the eighteenth century was profound, and most of its clergy espoused an enlightened moralism which had little room for religious emotion. Religious authority was based on "reasoned consent":

> Decades of responding to a distinct genre of Catholic apologetic that argued there could be no middle ground between Catholicism and scepticism had made most Anglican writers defensive of the power of human reason.[4]

For Deists faith was above all to be reasonable: belief in an all-powerful and dispassionate God who ruled over an orderly universe. Religion was primarily concerned with teaching obedience to the moral law, and this was the function of preaching. As a consequence the church to a considerable degree was not regarded as primarily a worshiping and praying community. The service of Holy Communion was neglected, while baptism was a private and perfunctory rite, not an incorporation into the community of the church. The architecture of churches built in colonial America reflected this change: the altar and baptismal font were put off to one side and the building was dominated by a pulpit and reading desk.

A revealing insight into the theological climate of the time comes from the theological reading list that Bishop William White of Philadelphia gave to the young John Henry Hobart in 1798 to help guide him in his studies. Scholar John Woolverton notes that "White was particularly concerned with forging a broadly unified view of the history of Anglicanism that could hold under a common umbrella of continuity the separate theological distinctions." Historical and theological continuity was hard to come by, and the list was decidedly eclectic, including Anglicans of every stripe whom White approved. Revealingly, the only Reformation thinker on the list was Richard Hooker; the moralistic and anti-Calvinist bias of eighteenth-century Anglicanism made the Reformation emphasis on sin and grace distasteful to White and his contemporaries. White's reading list for Hobart, moreover, came to define the theology of the Episcopal Church for years to come when it was authorized by the General Convention of 1804 as the "core curriculum" for a new generation of theological students.[5]

More serious was the effect of Deism on an Anglican theology of the Incarnation. At the time of the Reformation both Protestants and Catholics shared basic convictions about God and how human beings related to God. Both believed in God as a creator who not only had made the world, but continued to work in it—and in the lives of believers through the incarnation of Jesus Christ and the presence of the Holy Spirit. Despite their rejection of certain Catholic sacramental practices, Luther and Calvin certainly believed that God was actively present in the church and the world through scripture and the free gift of faith. For Hooker and the formularies of the Church of England, the incarnation of God in Christ was a fundamental Christian belief.

Against this, Deism called into question the very possibility of divine revelation, whether in Jesus Christ or in the Bible. It discounted the possibility of divine intervention through miracles, since the physical world was governed by immutable laws of nature—whether or not these laws originally came from the hand of God. Deism was a more complex movement than this brief summary suggests: it tried to make sense of radically new ideas introduced by the new science, Newtonian physics in particular, in ways that turned upside down customary ways of thinking about God and the world that had shaped Christian theology since the time of Plato and Aristotle.

The reaction to Deism in both England and America came in the form of an intense revivalistic movement that was transatlantic, cross-denominational, and transcended many racial and ethnic boundaries. Within the Church of England the evangelical revival began under the leadership of John Wesley, who appealed to religious experience and conversion, to God's awakening of the heart as well as the mind, with intense religious emotion as a sign of salvation. Preaching from scripture was an essential part of conversion: more than a collection of moral laws or questionable history, the Bible was the Word of God speaking to the human spirit through the Holy Spirit of God. It called for a conversion based upon a vital and living experience of God's presence. Conversion meant the acceptance of Jesus Christ as Savior, and it derived both from Bible reading and preaching "to the heart."

Both Wesley and his colleague George Whitefield brought the movement to America, where their itinerant preaching trips spread it through the colonies. Unlike other American Protestants, however, the rational and cautious Anglicans in America were little affected by the Great Awakening. Throughout the period of George Whitefield's preaching circuits through the colonies—he made seven in all—his fellow Anglican clergy preserved a united front against this form of religious enthusiasm which relied so heavily on dramatic experiences of conversion. It tended to exert greater appeal on Anglican lay people, some of whom broke with the Episcopal Church to become Baptists and, later, Methodists, when Methodism became a denomination separate from Anglicanism after the American Revolution.

One significant consequence, however, was the reemergence of a strong Evangelical movement in what would become the Episcopal Church. The evangelicals had always been a party within Anglicanism, emphasizing personal conversion through the atoning work of Christ's death on the cross and insisting on the importance of biblical preaching. In the Episcopal Church of the nineteenth century, the evangelical movement would be instrumental in the development of missionary work and social reform; in England, evangelicals such as William Wilberforce were outspoken in their opposition to British involvement in the slave trade in the Caribbean and the United States. Although several of the early leaders of the Oxford Movement were strongly influenced by Evangelicalism, the Evangelicals would eventually become a strong force in opposition to the Oxford Movement and the Catholic Revival, part of the renewal of Anglicanism which we shall be considering in the next chapter.

The Episcopal Church was on the road to becoming a distinct institution when the colonies declared their independence from the British crown, breaking the ties to England and the Church of England. A sufficient number of Anglicans remained in the former colonies for them to organize themselves into a new ecclesiastical body reflecting the independence of a new nation, founded upon different political principles. Monarchy was repudiated, and those who gathered to organize a new church after the war modeled its government on the newly formed government of the United States. They considered themselves no longer members of the Church of England, but part of an independent church in a new nation with its own form of government and its own *Book of Common Prayer.*

From the very beginning lay people had a central role in the governance of the Episcopal Church, as was true in all the other American churches except for the Roman Catholic. Bishops were to be elected by clergy and laity in all dioceses except Connecticut, where only ordained clergy could elect a bishop, and the congregation of each parish chose its own rector. Many Episcopalians in those early days remembered the "proud prelates" of England and wanted to make sure that bishops and priests would not have too powerful a role in the new church.

Thus from its beginning the Episcopal Church differed in some dramatic ways from the Church of England and from other European churches, whether Roman Catholic or Protestant, which were closely identified with the governing authorities. In the new context of American pluralism, the Episcopal Church remained one religious organization among many, and it had to be able to govern and support itself. As we shall see, these political changes would have considerable importance later when the Episcopal Church began to struggle with its theological identity and mission in the vastly more complex society that developed in the United States in the years after independence.

Despite this break with the past, the leaders of the Episcopal Church in the new American nation were also firm in their conviction that the Episcopal Church should not depart in other fundamental or significant ways from their traditional roots in the Church of England. The name "Episcopal," a venerable term dating from the seventeenth-century struggles with English Puritans, signified the belief that to be in line with apostolic succession a church must be governed by bishops *(episcope)* and uphold three distinct orders of ministry. This principle was enshrined in William White's *The Case of the Episcopal Churches in the United States Considered,* which acknowledged the historic orders of bishops, priests, and deacons but also held that the church was to be governed democratically through councils of clergy and laity. When Episcopalians from the churches of the former colonies met at General Convention in 1789, White's principles were upheld. It was made clear in the preface of the first *Book of Common Prayer,* furthermore, that the new church was not an upstart church, but a new form of the Church of England.

The preface made two important assertions. First, it declared that "when in the course of Divine Providence, these American States became independent with respect to civil government, their ecclesiastical independence was necessarily included." It then went on to say that "this church is far from intending to depart from the Church of England in any essential point of doctrine, discipline, or worship, or further than most local circumstances require." In making these two points about political change and theological continuity, the infant Episcopal Church did much the same thing that the Church of England had done at the time of its separation from Roman jurisdiction: it asserted the freedom of a national church to change as a new situation requires, while maintaining continuity with the essential beliefs and practices of the tradition it has received.

Significantly different, however, was the way this dynamic of continuity and change worked out over time. We have already seen how sixteenth-century theologians such as Richard Hooker sought to justify Anglicanism both to the Roman Catholics and to other Protestants. In the United States, however, little significant theological work was done until the end of the nineteenth century. The one exception was Samuel Johnson of Yale College, a Congregationalist who converted to Anglicanism, but his theological work made no great impression at the time and it is still relatively unknown today. In other words, the Episcopal Church differed from the rest of American Protestant Christianity not because of its theology, but in the way it organized itself. The tension of continuity and change was expressed primarily in political and social terms as the church struggled to find its place in the experiment of American democratic institutions.

This struggle focused on who would govern the new church and how bishops should be created. After the Revolutionary War, the Episcopal Church secured a bishop of its own through the consecration of Samuel Seabury of Connecticut by bishops of the Scottish Episcopal Church, but the fact that Seabury had been a British chaplain and still drew a pension from the British government made him unacceptable to the southern churches. In turn the New England churches disapproved of the churches in former colonies like Virginia and New Jersey because of the power they gave to the laity. Throughout the new Episcopal Church the power of bishops was carefully limited, however, so from the beginning a tension existed between the bishops, who claimed apostolic authority to teach, and the laity, who had an equal voice in determining ecclesiastical policy. Unlike the bishops of the Church of England, American bishops did not have the financial support of the government; like the clerical leadership of all the other American denominations, they had to establish their own authority both in teaching and in administrating the church. The chronic tension between laity and ordained leadership came to the fore in the decades following the Revolution as the Episcopal Church struggled to develop a clear sense of its identity and mission in a new context, where the structures of power and authority had radically changed.

By 1792 the Episcopal Church was a distinct denomination. It was to have an especially difficult time at the end of the eighteenth century, when a shortage of revenue, shrinking numbers of clergy, and a still evolving ecclesiastical organization meant that the church was initially ill-equipped to revitalize or renew itself. With the rise of a new generation of leadership in the nineteenth century, however, new growth and change began. It is to that new generation and its work of renewal we now turn.

Chapter 3

The Renewal
of Anglicanism

Throughout Christian history the Holy Spirit has stirred
anew in the church at times when neglect and lethargy
have held sway, and a new sense of commitment to the
gospel has emerged. The Reformation itself is one such
time; for Anglicanism, the nineteenth century is another.
By the end of the century, Anglicanism was transformed
as a result of its awakening to a renewed commitment to
making its mark on the social, intellectual, and theological
developments of the time. During that century the Episcopal Church discovered within itself three sources of vitality:
the Evangelical movement, with its emphasis on personal
piety, outreach, and mission; its rich Catholic past, which
for the leaders of the Catholic Revival opened up new
possibilities for the future; and the Broad Church movement, which emphasized the presence of God within larger
cultural, intellectual, and social advances.

The consecration in 1811 of John Henry Hobart and
Alexander Viets Griswold as bishops of New York and of
the Eastern Diocese (all of New England save Connecticut)
ushered in a new era and a new generation of church
leadership. John Henry Hobart stood for the high church

party in the Episcopal Church, while Griswold came out of the Evangelical movement. The extremely rational brand of Anglicanism exemplified by William White and his contemporaries had given way to new forms of identity for the Episcopal Church represented by these two men. High churchmen like Hobart saw the episcopate, priesthood, and sacraments as the principal means of grace. They believed that the Episcopal Church was a reformed but still Catholic Church where the apostolic order of bishops, priests, and deacons continued and the ancient catholic faith of the early church was preserved. Griswold and his contemporaries William Meade and Richard Channing Moore stressed the evangelical virtues of conversion of heart, personal discipline, and evangelism. Evangelical preachers and domestic missionaries,[1] though not as concerned about the catholic and sacramental heritage of the Episcopal Church, were nevertheless convinced that the gospel of Christ's death on the cross could be most effectively preached in the Episcopal Church. Teaching salvation through the power of the atonement and new birth, these Evangelicals were instrumental not only in reviving decaying Episcopal churches but in making the Episcopal Church attractive to other American Protestants.

In 1821 the General Convention created the Domestic and Foreign Missionary Society and the first missionary work of the church on the western frontier began, though early attempts to carry the Episcopal Church to the new territories in the west were disorganized and few. In some of the eastern dioceses, such as Virginia, Evangelical bishops had brought new vigor to their churches, but the significant change began in 1835, when the General Convention voted

to send bishops as missionaries to newly formed missionary districts in the west. As church historian David Holmes
remarks, the great significance of this decision was that it
was a return to the New Testament model of the episcopate:
bishops as apostles, rather than simply as heads of established congregations.[2]

The first appointed missionary bishop was Jackson
Kemper. An assistant at Christ Church, Philadelphia, under
Bishop William White, Kemper was ordained bishop in
1835 and immediately set off for the Northwest Territory.
During his episcopate he traveled on horseback throughout
Wisconsin, Indiana, Minnesota, Iowa, Missouri, Kansas,
and Nebraska, establishing numerous schools and churches
in towns (like Portage, Wisconsin) where the Episcopal
Church had been unknown. This new sense of mission was
driven by theological considerations as well as sociological
movements, and Jackson Kemper himself was of the high
church party. His sense of mission derived from his belief
that such a church offered a sacramental way that was
essential to the Christian life.

In 1841 he was joined by three newly ordained deacons
from The General Theological Seminary, John Henry Hobart, Jr., James Lloyd Breck, and William Adams. Working
with the European settlers as well as with the Native
Americans living in the territories, they founded a mission
in the woods of Wisconsin that later became the theological
seminary Nashotah House. The two small wooden buildings in which the early missionaries lived and worked there
still stand. Toward the middle of the century, James Lloyd
Breck went on to found a Native America mission to the
Chippewa in Minnesota.

Kemper's move to the west began the social transformation of the Episcopal Church and gave it a sense of mission
beyond its origins in the Church of England. The "non-Eng-

lish" Episcopalians of the nineteenth-century frontier (German, Swedish, and Polish settlers as well as Native Americans) opened the door for others to turn to the Episcopal Church: West Indians, who continued in their Anglican allegiance after moving to the United States, Hispanics from Mexico and the Caribbean, and Eastern Europeans who had been members of one of the Orthodox churches. They also prepared the church for work with the immigrants from Europe who arrived in the United States later in the century. Many Episcopal churches in the seaport cities of the east coast established charitable missions for Europeans, as did those on the west coast for Asian workers building the railroads across the continent. During the nineteenth century the Episcopal Church ceased to be "that English Church."[3]

Social reform, education, care for the poor, and personal reform were at the forefront of the Evangelical witness in the Church of England. The movement began in the hamlets and mining villages of England and Wales early in the eighteenth century and grew both in numbers and influence throughout the 1820s and 1830s, including such figures as William Wilberforce, Hannah More, John Newton, and the members of the Clapham Sect, who lived comfortable but simple lives and held to a personal rule of prayer and devotion. In England the Evangelicals were key figures in the Sunday school movement, the struggle to better the conditions in the factories, and the efforts to abolish slavery.

Their American counterparts also worked to educate slaves in the south before the Civil War. During the colonial period, in which Anglicanism was the established religion, most African American converts were members of the Church of England. Episcopal Evangelicals developed a benevolent ministry to the slaves and made efforts to evangelize African Americans during the years before the Civil War, but in the post-bellum period most African Americans preferred to join Methodist and Baptist churches. In the north, churches were formed among free African Americans, the earliest of which was St. Thomas African Episcopal Church, founded in Philadelphia in 1794. Absalom Jones, ordained to the priesthood in 1802, was perhaps its most famous pastor.

The 1820s and 1830s in America were the decades of the great Evangelical bishops, who built up their dioceses, founded seminaries, and were prominent in the founding of benevolent and educational societies. Perhaps one of the most striking of these was Richard Channing Moore, consecrated bishop of Virginia in 1814, when the diocese was on the verge of fading into oblivion. Moore was tireless in traveling and preaching throughout his diocese, reviving older parishes while planting new ones, and greatly improving the morale of his clergy. "He began with seven clergy," John Booty writes, "and at his death there were one hundred."[4]

The Catholic Revival, which also started in the early nineteenth century, began as a movement among Oxford dons (hence its other name, "the Oxford Movement") who wrote a series of *Tracts for the Times* deploring the state of the church and calling for a return to the doctrinal traditions and practices of the ancient church. Richard Hooker was an especially important source for the Tracts, but so too were the theologians of the patristic church.[5] The Oxford Movement was particularly important for its vision of the church as a divine society and hence the leaders of the Oxford Movement taught the centrality of the sacraments for the Christian life.

The dramatic and definite beginning of the Catholic Revival in England was the preaching of John Keble's Assize Sermon in Oxford in 1833. Parliament had threatened to abolish certain dioceses in Ireland because they were, as we would say now, "unproductive." In reply, Keble asserted that the Church of England answered to a higher authority, namely, Christ, who founded the church and the apostles, as well as their successors, the bishops, who governed it. The church, in other words, was a divine society not subject to the authority of the state. Its authority sprang from Christ and the apostles and, through apostolic succession, this authority rested on the bishops. Bishops were ultimately responsible only to Christ, not to Parliament.

This was a radical contention for the Church of England, which had originally separated from papal authority at the will of Henry VIII and since then had acknowledged the king as head of the church. Theologians like Keble, Edward Pusey, and John Henry Newman wanted to free the Church of England from secular control at a time when the almost mystical union of king (or queen, during the reign of Victoria) and church no longer existed and church affairs were now in the hands of parliamentarians. Keble and Pusey were attempting, therefore, to restore to the Church of England an older authority than king or pope, one that claimed continuity with the apostolic church through the historic succession of bishops.

In the Episcopal Church the onset of the revival was less dramatic. Many of the principles of the Tracts had been held by significant leaders in the American church since colonial times. Samuel Seabury, for example, had been consecrated the first bishop of the Episcopal Church by bishops of the Scottish Episcopal Church, which had maintained the older traditions represented by the Caroline divines. Moreover, the divisions between "high" and "low," "catholic" and "evangelical" were less pronounced than in the Church of England. It was not until later in the nineteenth century that Episcopal Church battles over ritual and piety became intense and highly polemical.

The context for these debates was also different. Far from being under state control, the Episcopal Church had no political or social claim to authority or preeminence beyond its wealth and its English heritage. The high church party of Hobart and Kemper claimed an episcopal authority deriving from the ancient church of the apostles. It was this claim, they thought, that set them apart from the sectarian churches that had sprung up in America and, because it assured their continuity in doctrine, from the more established Protestant churches like the Presbyterian, Lutheran, and Methodist. They also laid claim, over against the Roman Catholic Church, to a reformed Catholicism, just as Hooker did.

The Catholic Revival also recalled the church to its identity as a divine society with a sacramental relationship to God expressed primarily through baptism and the eucharist. This identity set Anglicanism apart from both the eighteenth-century Deist understanding of the church and from the churches of the Reformation. The Tractarians and their American counterparts believed that through the church as an apostolic community we become sons and daughters of God through the grace of the Incarnation.[6] Indeed, one writer went so far as to call the church "the extension of the Incarnation," the spiritual presence now of the Incarnate Christ.[7]

There was, of course, much more to the Catholic Revival, especially its revival of the religious life, its emphasis upon the spiritual life, and its restoration of ritual practices from ancient sources. However, the chief contribution of the Catholic Revival to the development and transformation of Anglicanism was the new self-understanding to which it led. Anglicans in the Church of England could no longer think of the church as simply a civil and political institution in society supporting the status quo. Anglicans in the Episcopal Church could no longer continue to think of the church as a quasi-established church for the rich and powerful, nor as a church that derived its prestige and authority from its English origins. Both churches had to begin asking what it meant to be catholic—catholic both as making universal claims and as claiming continuity with the doctrinal tradition of the apostolic church of the first several centuries of Christian history.

Like any other movement, the Catholic Revival had a negative side as well. Its original leaders stood against many of the changes brought about by new science and modern scholarship, for at the University of Oxford they were socially and intellectually isolated. Pusey, for example, a man of mammoth scholarship, once remarked that he had never in his life met anyone who was not a member of the Church of England! In the Episcopal Church, the leaders of the Catholic Revival joined a conservative reaction against many of the new religious movements such as Methodism and revivalism. Many rejected the new critical and historical study of the Bible as well as Darwin's theories about human evolution and development. They encouraged a romantic and nostalgic attitude toward the past, especially the Middle Ages, a nostalgia revealed by the theology, church architecture, liturgy, and piety that emerged. In our time Anglo-Catholics have often been slow to accept changes like the ordination of women, revisions of the *Book of Common Prayer*, the involvement of Anglicans in political and social movements, and ecumenism.

～

The later decades of the nineteenth century brought Anglicans in England and America face to face with a changed understanding of the church's relationship to the wider culture, which was increasingly dominated by the new science. In the nineteenth century the shift in understanding from the religious to the scientific and secular affected every area of society, not merely the intellectual. Furthermore, the rise of industry in both Britain and America resulted in large movements of the population away from farms and small towns into the crowded cities, with accompanying shifts in social and economic power. Yet the major challenge—or as some then saw it, the biggest threat—facing all Christian believers focused initially upon the authority of Holy Scripture. It was only the beginning of an ongoing struggle with questions we are asking today with no less urgency: How are we to understand the Bible and its authority?

Like other American Christians, Episcopalians believed that the words of the Bible were divinely inspired; therefore scholarly study of the books of the Bible—their sources, dates, authors, and historical accuracy—called these beliefs into question. When biblical critics used the new "higher criticism" from Germany to analyze how writings from different historical periods reflected quite different, often conflicting, theological points of view, it was no longer possible to assume that Moses wrote the first five books of the Bible, or that Genesis could give us the exact date of the creation of the world. The work of these scholars also exposed inaccuracies in accounts of historical events, such as the Flood and the Exodus, and showed that at least three different authors were responsible for composing the book of Isaiah. Furthermore, the so-called prophecies of the Hebrew scriptures were actually interpretations of contemporary events rather than predictions of the coming of Christ, as Christians had always thought. In other words, historical criticism of the Hebrew scriptures exposed Anglicans, along with everyone else, to the fact that the Bible had been written and edited, developed and changed by people, over the course of many centuries.

Such challenges to the Old Testament were difficult enough, and they became even more threatening when historical criticism was applied to the New Testament, calling both its historicity and uniqueness into question. Did all of the events reported in the New Testament actually happen? Did Jesus perform miracles of healing, and did he really walk on water? Even more, were the stories of his birth and bodily resurrection true and believable? Were all such "supernatural" events credible in a scientific age? And as scholars gained a greater knowledge of the religions of the ancient world, was it still possible to believe in the uniqueness of the Christian revelation? Some radical critics even doubted the historical existence of Jesus himself, and argued that the whole Christian faith was made up by St. Paul! Add to that the publication of Charles Darwin's theories about the evolution of human beings from apes—theories that not only challenged the book of Genesis but outraged nineteenth-century church members who believed themselves created in the "image of God"—and it is easy to see that mid-century Anglicans, along with other Christians, were heading into some deep and fast-moving currents.

Many Christians responded by holding even more firmly to what they had always been taught. The Roman Catholic Church condemned the new theories and began to expel those who accepted and taught them—Modernists, they were called—from its seminaries. A number of Protestant churches asserted the inerrancy of scripture no matter what scientific and historical evidence there might be to the contrary. And many people simply rejected the Bible altogether, dismissing all Christian claims to the truth.

The first Anglican response to what was certainly a crisis of faith was a collection of essays produced by the "liberal" wing of the Church of England called *Essays and Reviews*. Not only did the authors accept biblical criticism and the new scientific discoveries with enthusiasm, they also seemed to disregard the need for any historical foundation for Christian belief, emphasizing instead the need for a more "spiritual religion."

The American House of Bishops formally condemned *Essays and Reviews* in 1860, but these essays gradually became a rallying point for Anglicans on both sides of the Atlantic in what became the Broad Church movement, with its quest for intellectual rigor and desire to assimilate the new scholarship and view of the world into Anglican theology. It was part of a magnificent effort to understand how God works in history and how the truth of God in Christ incorporates all human truth, no matter how alien it may seem at first. They saw God at work not only in the transformation of human beings but also of the culture in which they live. The Episcopal Theological School in Cambridge, Massachusetts was an intellectual center for Broad Church scholarship, and churchmen like Phillips Brooks, William R. Huntington, and Thomas March Clark exemplified its attitude of mind.

A more formidable response to the new learning came later, which took the form of another collection of essays entitled *Lux Mundi: A Series of Studies in the Religion of the Incarnation*, published in 1889. It was edited by Charles

Gore, who was later to become bishop of Oxford and a major writer on theological and biblical questions. He and the other contributors were inheritors of the Catholic Revival whose theological work had moved beyond the rather narrow confines of the Tractarians. The authors of *Lux Mundi* accepted the challenge of historical and scientific criticism and attempted to respond from within the Christian tradition. It is, therefore, a highly successful attempt to answer to the question behind much Anglican thinking: how can Christian belief remain faithful to its past while embracing the present and future? The methodology these theologians developed for answering that question is expressed most succinctly in Gore's preface to the first edition:

> The real development of theology is...the process in which the Church, standing firm in her old truths, enters into the apprehension of the new social and intellectual movements of each age: and because "the truth makes her free," is able to assimilate all new material, to welcome and give its place to all new knowledge, to throw herself into the sanctification of each new social order, bringing forth out of her treasures things new and old, and showing again and again her power of witnessing under changed conditions to the catholic capacity of her faith and life.

The essays that follow carry out this principle of theological development in discussions about the doctrine of God, the Incarnation and its relation to scientific knowledge, the church and the sacramental life, and the inspiration of scripture. Their incarnational methodology showed a way for Anglicans at the end of the last century and the beginning of our own to think through the new questions in a way that was both catholic and critical.

Lux Mundi represented a new dimension in Anglican theology, one that was more distinctly catholic and incarnational. The book had an enormous impact not only in England but in the Episcopal Church as well, where its approach dominated the theological debate in most of the Episcopal seminaries. It was of particular significance in the long teaching and writing career of William Porcher DuBose, a creative incarnational theologian whose vision drew equally on the New Testament and the sacraments. In the next several generations, clergy found in the theology of *Lux Mundi* a rich resource for pastoral ministry, while religious scholars found a way to remain faithful to the Christian tradition even while taking seriously the enormous changes of the twentieth century.

Chapter 4

Mission and the Anglican Communion

When a community such as the Episcopal Church looks beyond its own doors in order to engage in mission, it has to confront more than the problems that arise out of its own history and worship. This turning to the work of mission has taken several forms in Anglicanism; it is not limited to evangelizing people for the church or even converting them to Christian faith. Broadly speaking, mission is part of our conviction that the church is called to witness to the Incarnate Christ in all the conditions of human existence, including politics and economics, war and peace, literature and the arts, and in the natural world we inhabit.

In this century, Episcopalians have turned outward in three important areas: the responsibility of the church in the social order, the ecumenical movement, and the radical challenge presented by the growth and diversity of the Anglican Communion, which reveals Anglicanism in strikingly different contexts. These three challenges have called us beyond ourselves to examine some of our old assumptions and to face new situations. In all three areas our belief in the Incarnation is central: how we are to witness to

Christ as Lord by accepting the fact that God is always calling the church into a new place and a new understanding of what it is in the midst of change.

In 1923 Frank Weston, Bishop of Zanzibar and a leading Anglo-Catholic, gave an address to the Anglo-Catholic Congress that bore witness to the social principles of the Catholic Revival:

> You have got your Mass, you have got your Altar, you have begun to get your Tabernacle. Now go out into the highways and hedges where not even the Bishops will try to hinder you. Go out and look for Jesus in the ragged, in the naked, in the oppressed and sweated, in those who have lost hope, in those who are struggling to make good. Look for Jesus. And when you see him, gird yourselves with his towel and try to wash their feet.[1]

The theology inspired by *Lux Mundi*, with its emphasis upon the Incarnation and strong sense of God's activity in history, awoke in many Anglicans of the late nineteenth century a realization that all the social structures and institutions of society are subject to Christ. They began to see that an incarnational faith calls for the transformation of the "secular" or "political" world in Christ, a transformation for which all Christians must take responsibility. Anglicans owe much of this vision of the church as the fulfillment of the whole social and political order to F. D. Maurice, Broad Churchman, prophet, and reformer whose social theology was shaped both by the Chartists and other revolutionary movements of 1848 and by the wretched conditions of the British working poor. In his greatest work,

The Kingdom of Christ, Maurice argues that the Incarnation is the definitive sign of God's incorporation of all human beings into the Kingdom. The church is both sacramental sign and instrument of the transformation of human society. Maurice also believed that the importance of the Incarnation for the Anglican understanding of the relationship between God and the church expresses a truth about God as Trinity of Persons and God's plan for all human beings:

> My desire is to ground all theology upon the name of God the Father, the Son, and the Holy Ghost, not to begin from ourselves and our sins; not to measure the straight line by the crooked one. This is the method I have learned from the Bible. There everything proceeds from God; he is revealing himself; He is acting, speaking, ruling.[2]

A founder of the Christian Socialist movement and professor at King's College, London, Maurice's liberal ideas and practical schemes made him very unpopular with the Church of England establishment. Dismissed from King's College in 1854 for advancing the radical notion of universal salvation, Maurice went on to found the Working Men's College in London, which offered a broad education in the humanities to working people. Education became his chief area of activity. Maurice saw very early the need for some kind of national education scheme and thought the Church of England should be at the forefront of this effort. But what underlay both his theology and his efforts at reform was the conviction that there is absolutely no distinction between "secular" and "sacred" and that "Christ is the head of *every* man, woman, and child."[3]

Maurice's theological vision had considerable impact upon a number of leading figures of the Episcopal Church, including Phillips Brooks, one of the greatest preachers of his day, and social prophets like Vida Dutton Scudder, James and Frederick Huntington, and William Dwight Porter Bliss, who involved the church in the newly emerging labor union movement. In this chapter we will consider two social thinkers in the modern Episcopal Church who represent different approaches to this question of the church's responsibilities to the social order.

Vida Scudder and William Stringfellow were of very different theological temperaments—Scudder had her roots in Anglo-Catholicism, while Stringfellow tended more to the evangelical—but each looked to belief in the Incarnate Christ as the source from which they could call for change. Vida Scudder carried on Maurice's tradition of Christian Socialism, while William Stringfellow was more at home with the evangelical and dialectical theology of Karl Barth. He was a sharp critic of the Episcopal Church and the American political system at the time of the Civil Rights movement and the Vietnam War—a time when the church, he thought, was accommodating itself to the "principalities and powers" governing the world. Stringfellow thought of himself as a reluctant Episcopalian, but found in the Episcopal Church a spiritual home that nourished him in an incarnational theology and the sacramental life. The fundamental conviction that each shared, although they derived it from different sources, was the prophetic importance of the Incarnation carried out in the sacramental life.

Born to a wealthy Congregationalist family in Boston, Vida Scudder became an Episcopalian under the tutelage of Phillips Brooks, rector of Trinity Church in Boston. After graduating from Smith College in 1881 Scudder and her mother traveled in Europe and ended up in Oxford where, her biographer writes, "Vida experienced a double awakening: she embraced Anglo-Catholicism, and John Ruskin made her a radical."[4] After her return to the United States, Scudder taught literature at Wellesley College and wrote extensively on the relationship between literature and Christianity. She became a socialist in 1889 after reading *Fabian Essays*. With several friends she worked in settlement houses for the immigrants who had begun to pour into the East Coast cities, identified herself with the nascent labor movement in 1893, and worked in slum parishes in Boston. She was also involved in the founding of the Society of the Companions of the Holy Cross, a religious community for academic women who were interested in the development of the spiritual life and social reform. Later in her life she wrote, "I was a Fabian with a difference, for the ultimate source of my socialism was and is Christianity. Unless I were a socialist, I could not honestly be a Christian."[5]

Scudder's socialism thus took an unusual turn from Fabianism and Marxism. It was distinctly religious, both sacramental and incarnational, derived from the tradition of *Lux Mundi*. Like Gore, Vida Scudder was no philosophical idealist who ignored the material dimensions of life and the economic realities of society. In *Socialism and Character* (1912), she wrote:

> The Christian who is also a socialist can say that, despite superficial appearances to the contrary, it has really been the belief in the Incarnation working in the depths...that has led the western nations on to their present strong and clear demand for the rehabilitation of the natural order....Belief that the spirit must and can be revealed only through the instrument of the flesh is natural to one who has knelt at Bethlehem.[6]

At the same time, however, Vida Scudder balanced the doctrine of the Incarnation with a deep awareness of the reality of human sin and the need for the sacrifice and atonement which are to be found in the cross of Christ. She was, thus, no advocate of essential human goodness or the inherent perfectionism of human nature, as she made clear in *Socialism and Character:*

> Christ gives us the clear and fearless statement that in a dislocated and imperfect world not only must growth be fostered, but catastrophe must be watched for and welcomed. Judgment as well as progress is essential to the furtherance of the Kingdom of God.[7]

In this way, Scudder stood in the tradition of Bishop Gore and others of the *Lux Mundi* tradition: the Incarnation is the foundation on which we bring about change in society and the church, for Christ reveals to us both God's judgment and our hope.

Until her death in 1954 Vida Scudder was a quiet but powerful force in the lives of many Episcopalians, especially the women with whom she worked in settlement houses and workers' institutes in Boston and New York, and those who read her articles and books. Though at the time she was not well known beyond the small circle of women who worked with her for social justice, in many ways she typified the increasing involvement of women in the active life of the Episcopal Church. In her writings and life she witnessed to the theological foundation for social justice in the Incarnation and the sacraments.

William Stringfellow had quite a different impact on the Episcopal Church of the twentieth century. While he was in some ways a prophet without honor in his own country—he was often dismissed by academics as "a lay theologian"—he was widely known, much in demand as a speaker and author on issues facing church and society. Though he was a life-long Episcopalian, his relationship to the church was always tangential because he was sharp in his criticisms of what he thought were the church's failures as an institution to live out the gospel of the Incarnation. He believed that the Incarnation expressed most fully God's judgment upon all the powers of society to which the church too often accommodates itself.

After graduation from Harvard Law School in the late 1950s, Stringfellow worked as an attorney in Harlem and, while living there, became convinced that the most significant way to deal with the problems of poverty lay in scripture and worship, grounded in the doctrine of the Incarnation. In *My People Is the Enemy*, which was a reflection upon his time in East Harlem, he wrote:

> The Christian faith is not about some god who is an abstract presence somewhere else, but about the living presence of God here and now, in this world, in *exactly* this world, as men know it and touch it and smell it and live and work in it....The meaning of Jesus Christ is that the Word of God is addressed to me, to *all* men, in the very events and relationships, any and every one of them, which constitute our existence in this world. That is the theology of the Incarnation.[8]

For Stringfellow the Incarnation meant that in Christ "there is a radical and integral relationship" between God and humankind; the reconciliation of the world in Christ established humanity that was "in unity with both God and the whole world." In the sacraments of the worshiping community Stringfellow saw the representation and enactment of that unity:

> When a congregation gathers in sacramental worship, the members of the Body are offering the world to God, not for His sake, not for their own sake, but for the sake

of the world, and the members then and there celebrate God's presence in the world, and on behalf of the world, even though that world does not yet discern His presence.[9]

Thus the representation of the gospel in the sacraments was a political act, one directed to the transformation of society:

> The Christian political witness is the audacity to trust that God's love for this world's existence is redeeming, so Christians are human beings free to live in this world by grace in all practical matters and decisions. That is why the Church of Christ is the only society in this world worthily named great.[10]

Like Vida Scudder, Stringfellow lived out his incarnational beliefs by working with the poor and displaced until his health forced him to retire. After that he continued to work out the political implications of the Incarnation by his defiance of the "principalities and powers," speaking out strongly against the American involvement in Vietnam and Christian complacency toward the war. He did not see the Incarnation as an idealistic doctrine concerned only with "other-worldly" matters; rather, the Incarnation is God's judgment upon both church and society.

In this brief look at both of these social prophets, one in the early decades of this century, the other closer to our own time, we can see, I believe, how the doctrine of the Incarnation, so fundamental to Anglicanism, can still lead to the continuing transformation of the Episcopal Church from its captivity to complacency and conformity. Stringfellow was one who moved the Episcopal Church to begin to face the realities of American society after World War II and to challenge it to change. But he, like Vida Scudder, did so from within a belief that what God has revealed in Christ is the only means for genuine renewal and change. The Incarnation is the reality of the church which allows for change within the continuity of what God makes known to us in Christ.

A second area of mission in the twentieth-century Episcopal Church is our ecumenical conversations with other churches. From those conversations we have been shown much about God and about ourselves, and we now see more clearly what we can learn from other Christian traditions and what our mission within the larger church may be. For a deepening sense of mission should not be limited to evangelism of the unchurched: it should also mean moving out of those assumptions and beliefs that hinder witness to the gospel. Increasingly, as our conversations have progressed, we have seen what our commitment to the heritage of Anglicanism means and have been called into a new form of witness with other Christian communities.

The changes began for us, once again, in the nineteenth century. Meeting in Chicago in 1886, the House of Bishops approved a statement that defined what the principles of unity should be between the Episcopal Church and other churches. The Chicago Quadrilateral, as it was called, originated in a book by William Reed Huntington, *The Church Idea: An Essay Towards Unity*, published in 1870. Huntington proposed that the Episcopal Church move beyond its English heritage and seek to become the foundation for the Catholic (but non-Roman) Church in America. His sentiments were basically establishmentarian: he thought that the Protestant Episcopal Church was the kind of religious institution around which a right-thinking nation would unite. The Quadrilateral went through various changes until it was finally accepted by the Lambeth Conference in 1888 and became known as the Chicago-Lambeth Quadrilateral.[11]

With certain modifications, this document has remained the basis for all of our subsequent conversations with other churches. It lists four doctrinal points that define what is essential for our continuity as a church with the apostolic church of the first centuries and which, consequently, must form the basis for our unity with other churches. First, the Holy Scriptures are the revealed Word of God and provide "the rule and ultimate standard of faith." Second, the Apostles' Creed and the Nicene Creed are the statement of Christian faith. Third, the sacraments of baptism and eucharist are ordained by Christ himself. Fourth, the historic episcopate, "locally adapted in the methods of its administration" according to the varying needs of the church, is the basis for the church's unity.

About the first three points of the Quadrilateral—Bible, creeds, and sacraments—there has been considerable consensus. The sticking point has been number four, the historic episcopate, understood by some Anglicans as an unbroken chain or "succession" that links the bishops and ministers of today with the earliest apostles. Many churches in the reformed tradition who would be quite happy to be one with us in respect to Bible, creeds, and sacraments refuse to accept the historic episcopate and its implication that their ministry is invalid and that their ministers and pastors would need to be "re-ordained." As a result, ecumenical conversations have often stalled on this point.

Justifications for the historic episcopate have had a checkered history in Anglicanism. At the time of the Reformation in England the episcopate was retained for political reasons as much as for theological ones. The Roman Catholic Church then and now insists that Anglican episcopal orders are invalid because the historic succession of bishops by the laying on of hands was broken. Anglicans have defended the succession, even though Richard Hooker argued that the ordained ministry of those churches without the historic succession could still be regarded as authentic—what in contemporary debates has been called "valid, but irregular." The earliest leaders of the Oxford Movement reasserted the necessity of apostolic succession in the episcopate in order to strengthen their understanding of the church as a divine society over against the state.[12]

Since the Revolutionary War, Episcopalians have been careful to maintain the historic episcopate as a sign of validity and continuity with the apostolic church. Clergy from denominations that lack the historic episcopate must be ordained by an Episcopal bishop when they become Episcopal priests. This is also true for other Anglican churches: apostolic succession in the historic episcopate is regarded as an essential element for any scheme of church union.

The question might well be asked, Why all the fuss? What is there about the historic episcopate that is so important that we would seemingly "unchurch" those perfectly good Christians who do not have it? Why do we insist upon it even when it becomes an impediment to the reunion of the churches?

The answer to those questions is complicated, tied up as it is with politics, self-identity, and a bit of pride and arrogance as well as our understanding of the nature of the church. Our ecumenical conversations have required of us a new appreciation of what apostolic succession in the historic episcopate means for us. Many Anglicans have argued that having bishops in succession to the apostles themselves through the laying on of hands *guaranteed* that the Anglican Church was truly a branch of the Catholic Church, alongside the Roman Catholics and the Orthodox, and that its sacraments were valid. As attractive as that view is, however, modern scholarship shows it to be historically unfounded and theologically misguided.

New Testament accounts of Jesus' commission to the apostles cannot be treated as though it were a blueprint for the church in successive generations. We can now see more clearly what the early church itself recognized: apostolic ministry means much more than a guarantee of validity. Apostolic succession means standing in the teaching and fellowship of the apostles, while the laying on of hands in historic succession is an outward sign of continuity in that teaching and fellowship, but no guarantee.

As a result our more intense and serious ecumenical conversations with the Lutheran churches, the General Convention of the Episcopal Church in 1982 adopted a resolution on "Principles of Unity" which, while reaffirming the Chicago-Lambeth Quadrilateral, also broadened its point about the historic episcopate.[13] This emendation also says much about theological development in the Episcopal Church itself—while it represents a change in our thinking, it is a development that stands firmly within the tradition we have received. It expresses our commitment to be faithful to the apostles' teaching and fellowship.

A growing awareness of the diversity within the Anglican Communion is another significant aspect of Anglicanism's development in this century. It has already led to fundamental changes in how we think of ourselves as Episcopalians, and this new knowledge has required that we deal with our mission not as a small body in the United States or as an offshoot of the Church of England, but as a church that includes vastly different cultures and ways of understanding our Christian expectations and responsibilities.

The roots of the Anglican Communion were planted by English colonists who took the Church of England with them to North America, as they did to Australia and New Zealand when those territories became extensions of the British empire. As the British empire grew and expanded in the nineteenth century, the Church of England went along with it, largely to minister to the spiritual and cultural needs of British settlers, politicians, and business people in Africa, Asia, and the Caribbean. The church was a bit of home-away-from-home for the English, and it is still possible to find church buildings in far-off places that look like the parish churches dotting the English countryside. The colonists also took with them the English ways of worship—the *Book of Common Prayer*, music, and liturgical practices—and the episcopal pattern of church government.

In some parts of the British empire nothing more happened; Anglicanism continued on as an extension of the Church of England. In others, however, missionaries from England preached the gospel to indigenous peoples and before anyone quite knew what was happening, Anglican Christianity had created flourishing national churches and an indigenous Anglicanism. The change and growth was so varied from place to place that no general pattern could be discerned until after World War II, when new nations emerged from the old British empire with new national churches.

The first indication that Anglicanism was no longer confined to the British Isles and North America was the meeting of Anglican bishops in London, at Lambeth Palace, the residence of the Archbishop of Canterbury, in 1867.

Since then Lambeth Conferences, which include all the bishops of the Anglican Communion, have met every ten years, except during World War II. Although the conferences have no legislative power for the national churches, issues of importance for all the churches of the Communion are discussed and important resolutions have been agreed upon. Until recently, those issues have been largely determined by the bishops from the more powerful churches in Britain, North America, Australia, and New Zealand. Now the bishops from Africa and elsewhere are beginning to push for a more comprehensive agenda about issues facing their churches, for example, evangelism, Christian and non-Christian relations, polygamy in Africa, and other problems of adaptation to non-western cultures.

The Anglican Communion developed as a fellowship of national and local churches without a unified structure of authority but with a strong sense of identity, even though that identity may be hard to define. The words "communion" and "fellowship" have considerable theological significance; both reflect a frequent theme in the New Testament expressed in the Greek word *koinonia*. *Koinonia* meant the fellowship which human beings ordinarily have with one another, but in the New Testament church the word took on a much deeper meaning: the communion Christians have in Christ and through Christ with God. This *koinonia* found its concrete expression in the congregations that Paul established through his missionary journeys. All those congregations—eventually to become churches in Rome, Corinth, and elsewhere—were united with one another, or were "in communion," not through any ecclesiastical or political structure, but through their common belief in Jesus Christ and in the gospel of salvation. In *koinonia* with Christ Christians found their *koinonia* with God. As theological reflection deepened this notion, *koinonia* came to mean our participation in the Holy Trinity, with the church a sign of the ultimate communion of all human beings in God.

So we are using a very rich and deep word when we speak of Anglicanism as a communion of churches. The Anglican Communion is not an accidental coming together of like-minded people, but a community or fellowship that we have in Christ that transcends our differences. Thus, while in their origins the national churches of Anglicanism did have a common cultural and political center in the Church of England, as they have developed into a worldwide communion they are becoming something more which is yet to be realized.

No one in the Anglican Communion really knows what the practical implications of our communion with one another may yet be in terms of working out what each national church does and how it hears the gospel. For example, the Episcopal Church in the United States now ordains women to the priesthood and episcopate, while some churches in Africa reject such ordinations. Similarly, Episcopalians deplore polygamy while the African bishops debate the possibility of permitting it within the church. If such disparate churches are willing to remain in communion, that in itself is an expression of the Incarnation. We Anglicans who are in communion with one another are having to ask how the gospel of Jesus Christ is to be incarnate in a particular time and place, and to a particular people and community. How do we enjoy continuity in our shared tradition of belief while still making room as new political and cultural situations arise?

These are not questions unique to Anglicanism, of course, for all Christians have been faced with them from the beginning. How can a Jew, from a particular time and place, be the Savior of the world? How did an essentially

Jewish religion adapt to the culture of the Roman empire? How does a "eurocentric" church, one shaped by western politics and thought, become indigenous in Asia or Africa? In other words, what does it mean for us to believe that God is present in human history in all its diversity? How can Christian mission be freed from its captivity to a particular culture, whether European, American, or English, so that others may hear the gospel of Jesus Christ? These are the questions with which Anglicans are now struggling, and they will become of even greater importance as we continue on. They will be another dimension in the transformation of Anglicanism in the twenty-first century.[14]

PART II

Anglican Belief and Practice

Chapter 5

Anglican Believing

That man from Portage has now heard something about the history of the Episcopal Church and even how it got to Portage. But perhaps the conversation between him and the young deacon went on, and he asked a more penetrating and difficult question: "Church history is all well and good, but what do Anglicans believe about God?" Indeed, he might have said, "I believe in God, but that doesn't mean I have to belong to a church. Churches are fine for people who like that kind of thing, but they don't have much to do with believing in God."

It would, of course, be perfectly possible to think of the Episcopal Church, or any other church for that matter, as just another institution in society, or as that familiar building on the corner. Churches own buildings, after all, and operate as businesses; they collect and spend money; they employ people and pay insurance premiums; and sometimes they do not seem all that different from other social gatherings of like-minded people. Yet the church is more than just another institution or business enterprise. As interesting as the history of Anglicanism may be, the important thing is that we are a church *because we believe in God*. It is our believing in God—not our history or our buildings—that is the reason for our existence.

Christians believe that the God in whom we believe has been revealed uniquely in the person and life of Jesus. Early in the history of the Christian church, such belief in Jesus Christ was expressed in the creeds and formulated by theologians as the doctrine of the Incarnation. That Jesus was incarnate as a human being and that he shares in our history and humanity remains a central belief of all Christian churches because it expresses what is essential to our faith: "For God so loved the world that he gave his only Son, so that everyone who believes in him may not perish but may have eternal life" (John 3:16).

The doctrine of the Incarnation also came to be of particular importance in the development of Anglicanism, affecting the way we think, pray, and worship to a degree that is unique within the larger Christian community. For us it has provided a link between the God in whom we believe and the church with which we believe, so it is important to see where the doctrine of the Incarnation comes from, how it developed as an expression of Christian belief, and how it has been central to the Anglican way of believing.

When we say in the creeds "We believe in God," we are trying to give expression to what concerns us most deeply about ourselves and our world: the beliefs and hopes and experiences that shape and form our lives as Christian people. Without our belief in God all of church history and theology would be simply an academic exercise, a study perhaps in the sociology of religion and its cultural influence. It is our belief in God that makes us *church*, a gathered community, and therefore any glimpse of the Anglican vision must begin with an understanding of what Anglicans mean when we say "We believe in God."

"God" is a complex word expressing many levels of meaning. Like other deep words—love, death, life, hope, justice, and joy, for example—it is a word that is hard to define but easy to use. We say that we believe in God, worship God, pray to God. We also say that we believe God to be somehow involved with what goes on in our world and in our lives. We feed the hungry and care for the sick and dying in the name of God, but in times of war we have also killed in the name of God—that is, for what we think is God's cause.

"Believing" is also a word with complex and varying meanings. For example, I can say that I believe some event occurred when I am not really sure that it did: "I believe that the car went through a red light, but I wouldn't want to swear to it in court." Or, "I believe what the astronomers tell me about the universe because they know more about it than I do." "Believing" can indicate uncertainty about whether something is true or not, or it can mean accepting something as true because someone I trust tells me so. We can believe many things what a politician says in an election year or what a preacher says on Sunday morning—but in many cases we do so, as we say, with a grain of salt.

We can also talk about "believing" in a much stronger sense. For example, to say that we believe *in* something or someone can express a basic or fundamental commitment; it can be an act that determines my life and shapes my future actions. Also, if a person I believe in tells me something of importance, then I am more inclined to accept it; I believe what she or he tells me because I have a basic commitment to that person. Of course, the commitment can be both good and bad. At one time many people believed in Stalin's version of Communism in the Soviet Union, but eventually lost faith in Stalinism when they saw its disastrous consequences.

Believing *in* someone or an idea has deeper consequences for one's life than simply believing that some event may or may not be true. "Believing in" involves commitment; "believing that" is open to modification should more information come our way. Of course, believing in a person or an idea can also be open to change, if the person turns out not to be the person we had thought, or the idea becomes destructive. All of us can be gullible from time to time, but to lose our belief in a person or idea is much more wrenching than just coming to believe that something else may be the case—that the car did go through the red light after all.

When we say the Christian creeds, we begin by saying that we believe *in* God, not just that we believe something *about* God. Even when we say that the God we believe in is creator of heaven and earth, for example, the fundamental commitment is to God; what we mean by "creator" is tied up with that more fundamental belief in God. We could well mean different things when we say we believe that God is "creator"—as shown by the ongoing conflict between "creationists" who believe God created the world in six literal days and scientists who have a very different timetable for the origins and evolution of the universe—but our belief that God is creator of heaven and earth is not dependent upon either the cosmological speculations of ancient peoples or the discoveries of contemporary astrophysicists. Our ability to say that we believe in God as creator of heaven and earth arises from our prior or more fundamental belief in God as the source and center of all that is, a belief to which the biblical story in Genesis bears profound witness.

Such distinctions, as obvious as they may be, are important for religion generally, but especially for Christian believing. Over the centuries Christians have believed many things about God or Jesus Christ or the Holy Spirit. A multitude of stories and teachings have developed in Christian tradition, some of which we today would no longer consider believable or edifying. Consider the wrathful and angry God of much "fire and brimstone" preaching that reflects many of the stories in the Hebrew scriptures about God's vengeance, or the more charming but equally disturbing stories in some of the apocryphal gospels (that is, the early writings that were rejected by the Christian community) about the young boy Jesus who cursed his playmates because they beat him in a game. Christian history is littered with those whose beliefs about God led them to kill or torture themselves or other people "in the name of God."

Over the years intelligent and devout Christians have sometimes quite legitimately disagreed about the way in which they would talk about God and God's relationship to them: Thomas Aquinas in the thirteenth century talked about God in different terms from those of Martin Luther in the sixteenth century. Today there is considerable controversy among Christian people about saying that God is "Father," since some believe that "Father" is a self-revealed name for God and so is not replaceable by any other name, while others, equally serious and devout, consider it a name that should no longer be used or used much more sparingly because it seems to imply that God is male. Both groups would say, however, that they believe in the God of Jesus Christ, even though they talk about God in different ways.

Ultimately, of course, all language about God is tentative, a "stuttering," as an early theologian put it. And Thomas Aquinas, who wrote volumes of books about God, said after a vision of God in prayer that everything he had written was "as straw," and he withdrew into silence. As one contemporary theologian, Karl Rahner, has said, God is Absolute Mystery, and Christian mystics have always reminded us that God is known in silence and the "dark night of the soul." This is one reason why we need poets, storytellers, and others with such gifts of imagination, as well as theologians and preachers, for believing in God is an act of commitment and of wonder and courage that calls us beyond ourselves into a greater reality than our words can ever express.

And yet we Anglicans, along with other Christians, dare to make a confession of belief in God every Sunday when we say one of the two creeds that we use in worship: the Apostles' Creed in the services of Morning or Evening Prayer or the Nicene Creed in the Holy Eucharist. We also baptize people with a confession of faith *in* God the Father Almighty, *in* Jesus Christ, and *in* the Holy Spirit. Whatever conflicts we may have about how we talk about God, we are still confessing that "we believe in" a certain kind of God. Who is this God of Jesus Christ in whom we believe?

The early followers of Jesus, so we are told in the first writings of the Christian community, came to believe that the "carpenter's son" whom they followed was more than an itinerant teacher and worker of wonders; he had some-thing to do with God. As Jews, the God they knew was the God present in the history of their people and one to whom they prayed in the community of Israel. The God with whom Jesus had to do was the God they knew from their own experience as good Jews. The teacher was crucified and died, and yet, as the first disciples believed, was still present with them in a new and astounding way, what they called resurrection.

Various communities took shape around this person; they remembered him, continued his teaching, and believed in his presence with them in those communities formed in his name by his Spirit. The stories about him and his teaching eventually came to be written down, and they make up what we call the New Testament—the gospel accounts and the letters Paul and others wrote to the churches which they had established throughout the Roman empire.

Soon also these small communities, each with its own set of beliefs and remembered stories, began to draw together and organize themselves. They developed liturgies for initiating new members into their community—baptism—and forms of worship that centered around Jesus Christ by remembering and recalling his death and resurrection—the eucharist. They brought together the various writings about Jesus and decided which were inspired by the Holy Spirit and were authentic presentations of him—the canon of Holy Scripture. In due course, also, some people in each community were set aside to minister to the community—deacons and priests—or to have oversight *(episcope)* of the various communities—what we now call bishops or chief pastors.

Gradually, and with a great deal of muddling through, all these writings, doctrines, and structures took on definite shape and developed into traditions and customs, some of central importance, such as those about Jesus himself, and some of minor importance, such as Paul's strictures about women covering their heads or men not having long hair. The irony of Christian history is that sometimes the minor customs have been a source of greater conflict than the major traditions of belief!

In due course, also, after much thinking and praying, arguing and debating, believing and worshiping, they began to give names to the events of Jesus' historical life and of his continuing presence with them in the community and to develop definite teachings about those events and about Jesus himself. The names and teachings have come down to us as doctrines—what we believe about the God whom he called Father, about Jesus himself, and about the Holy Spirit whom he had promised to send: the Holy Trinity, the Incarnation, the indwelling of the Holy Spirit, grace, and salvation.

Simply listed that way, doctrines about God can seem very off-putting: intellectual constructions that obscure a simple faith in Jesus. In fact, these doctrines were part of the early church's attempt to explain and preserve from distortion the story of what God had done and was continuing to do in Jesus. The development of doctrine was an integral part of the church's mission—telling the story of Jesus to others. Because the early disciples of Jesus preached his gospel in a world full of gods and divinities, where even the emperor was a god, it was important for them to get the story right, namely, that in "the carpenter's son" a new age had begun and the word of truth about God and human beings had been revealed.

Nowhere was this belief put more forcefully than in the prologue to the gospel of John:

> In the beginning was the Word, and the Word was with God, and the Word was God. He was in the beginning with God. All things came into being through him, and without him not one thing came into being....And the Word became flesh and lived among us, and we have seen his glory, the glory as of a father's only son, full of grace and truth....From his fullness we have all

received, grace upon grace. The law indeed was given
through Moses; grace and truth came through Jesus
Christ. (John 1:1-3, 14, 16-17)

When you believe such things about someone, it is important to get the story right.

In order to get the story right the early church produced
two creeds, two professions of faith. The earliest, the
Apostles' Creed, developed out of the early affirmations
used in baptism. When the candidates for incorporation
into the church were brought before the assembly, they
confessed their faith in God, the Father and Creator, in Jesus
the Son of God and Lord who was born of the Virgin Mary,
who died and rose again, who will come again in glory to
judge all that is, and in the Holy Spirit. The baptismal creed
is a simple and direct expression of faith, and it is still used
today in the baptismal liturgy and in the daily offices of
Morning and Evening Prayer.

The Nicene Creed was composed in the fourth century
during two councils of the early church that were called to
reconcile conflicting interpretations about the nature of
Jesus and his relationship to God the Father. The Arian
party believed that Jesus, in his divine nature, could not be
identified completely with the eternal and unchanging God.
To argue that Jesus' divinity is one with God's divinity
would make God, so to speak, less than God—too mixed up
with human history and the material world. They con-
cluded, therefore, that to call Jesus the "Son of God" must
mean something less than truly and completely divine,
something more like a mediator between the eternal nature
of God and the created nature of human beings.

The opposing party, led by Athanasius, held that if Jesus
is anything less than the true nature of the eternal God,
such a belief would have disastrous consequences for our

salvation in Christ. Only if Jesus is truly God, they argued, can human beings receive the gift of salvation and eternal life through his redeeming work. In order to be our savior, Jesus must be of "one being" or "one substance" with God the Father.

The Greek word they used was *homoousion*, a term difficult to translate into English; "one being" or "one substance" is the closest we can come. The basic point, however, is that this human being, who shares completely in our human nature, also shares completely in the divine nature and can truly be called God. He is not a demigod or lesser divinity (of which there were already quite a few in Greek and Roman religions), but he is one with the same God made known to the people of Israel, who makes and rules the whole creation.

Further theological reflection led the Council of Constantinople in 381 to include in the Creed of Nicea a similar confession of belief in the divinity of the Holy Spirit: "the Lord, the giver of life, who proceeds from the Father [and the Son]."[1] The final version of the Creed of Nicea became the basic confession of Christian faith and today is said every Sunday in the eucharist of the Episcopal Church as a theological statement of our belief in God.

The conflict about the nature of Jesus did not end there. The Council of Nicea left significant questions to be explored by future generations of Christians: Now that we confess that Jesus is truly God, truly one with the divine nature, what does this say about his human life? Is he truly a man, a human being like us, tempted as we are and suffering as we do, or does he only *appear* to be a human being, so that his life among us and his death were only a pretense? If he was not tempted as we are, then can he really save us? If he did not really suffer and die on the cross as a truly human person, then can his resurrection have any meaning for us?

The New Testament writings made it clear that Jesus was a human being, a man, with all the normal characteristics of our humanity: he was born of a human mother, grew up, walked about and talked with his disciples, ate, slept, got angry and tired, wept, and finally died. But the New Testament writings also made it quite clear that he was much more than just an ordinary human being, "an average guy," so to speak: his birth, according to some accounts, was miraculous; he performed miracles of healing and, much to the astonishment of his followers, he forgave people their sins; he taught the wisdom of God; in the gospel of John he was remembered as having identified himself with God and as having said that he would send the Spirit of God to be with his followers; and he was raised from the dead and taken up in glory to his Father in heaven.

Even more important, through prayer and worship the early Christians had come to believe in him as the Messiah of Jewish hopes and expectation, the Savior, the Son of God, one who was eternally begotten from God, and one who continued to be present with the community of believers who gathered to remember him in the Holy Eucharist. What was he? Who was he? Certainly more than a man pretending to be God, and certainly more than God pretending to be a man. And he was certainly not, as a confused preacher once described him, "half God and half man." Most important of all, Who is he now? In his glory "at the right hand of the Father" does he still share our humanity, so that we can continue to confess him as truly God and truly human?

In order to debate these questions another council was called in the city of Chalcedon in 451. Answers did not come easily, and it was only after much debate that the bishops and theologians resolved upon language for Christians to use in talking about their belief in Jesus as both God and human. They tried to express, however inadequately, the fundamental Christian mystery of belief in Jesus Christ, a man living in space and time who is the presence with us of the eternal and holy God.

In their Chalcedonian Definition (the text can be found on page 869 of the *Book of Common Prayer)* the bishops and theologians declared that when speaking of Jesus we should say that he is completely God and completely human *(anthropos* in Greek), consisting of a soul and body, of one substance *(homoousios)* with the Father and at the same time one substance with us, like us in every way, apart from sin. Jesus was begotten of the Father before all ages, and begotten for our salvation of Mary the Virgin, the God-bearer *(Theotokos)*. Thus we should confess him as "one and the same Christ, Son, Lord, Only-begotten" in two natures that form one person.

The mystery these words seek to clarify is that Jesus is one person, one individual. He is not somebody split in two—"half God and half man"; rather, he is a unity of all that is God and all that is human. Our hope for salvation is to be found precisely in his unity as a person, divine and human. Through him, as a human being, we human beings are united to God. Jesus Christ is God's presence with us in a completely human life.

What does all this theological language mean for us Christians? Let me try to explain it in terms of my own experience of living into the Incarnate Christ. Over the years I have learned that only in an offering of all that we are—our sins and failures as well as the good things about ourselves—can we find our ultimate union with God, what we call salvation or eternal life. I am able to offer my *self*, however hesitantly most of the time, only because through faith in Jesus I share in the life of one who was, like me, a complete human being with all the limitations of our humanity, but who in that human life showed also what it means to be one with God.

On the other hand, much of the time I am split apart, veering off in many different directions, uncertain about what I want and need, torn between my desire for God and the idolatry of self. My hope—and it is the hope of all human beings, I believe—is to be one self, one person, in a union of love with the Source of all that is and with my fellow human beings. Only then can I truly be myself.

I cannot, of course, read the minds of those who composed the Chalcedonian Definition, but I do believe that in their highly technical language we can hear the same hope. Our hope for salvation and eternal life is to be found in the person Jesus, who is one with God and one with us—not someone split asunder between a divine calling and a human existence, but one who showed us what life with God is like and who now makes it possible for us to share that life. Whatever language we may use to describe such a hope, whether it be that of Chalcedon or some other, this is the Christian belief in the Incarnation of God in Christ.

What kind of God we believe in—and the words and images we use to describe that God—has serious consequences for how we live our lives. Our image of God will affect how we pray and how we experience God's presence, what our moral principles are, and how our belief affects our everyday decisions about voting, eating and drinking, sexual practices, and all the rest. We all have convictions and prejudices that on the surface may seem to have very little to do with believing in God, but when we examine our convictions and prejudices more deeply we often discover that they are the consequence of deeper belief or unbelief in a certain kind of God.

The intellectual and emotional move from believing in God in a general sort of way to believing in a certain kind of God involves many factors. Like so many other such moves in a person's life—falling in love and committing your life to another person, for example—it can be the result of a person's education, ethnic origin, cultural background, the language one speaks, sexual orientation, gender, family status, and a host of other psychological, economic, and political factors. How we believe is not just a matter of good or bad theology. A person who has grown up with angry and abusive parents may have great difficulty in believing that God is loving and forgiving. A person who has lived in a society in which power and authority are exercised by only one group may well believe that God is their exclusive property. And there can be many other variations.

In other words, there are many different reasons for why and how we believe as we do. The days are long past when someone became a Christian because there were no viable religious alternatives. And certainly being an Anglican is no longer simply the consequence of the culture or class into which one falls by accident of birth. Most people nowadays make some kind of choice—a decision to believe or not to believe and a decision to believe in one way rather than another. The choice we make is important because it has consequences for who we are and who we are becoming.

As I said in the first chapter of this book, when I was recounting something of my own history with the Episcopal Church, I really did not have to choose to believe in the Christian God—such belief was part of the world in which

I grew up—and I more or less fell into the Episcopal Church by accident or, as I would like to believe, by the leading of God. I did not quite consciously choose it. But as I have gone on being an Anglican through the years, I have become more and more aware of why I remain with it. I do so not out of inertia or because it is pleasant and convenient, but because I believe that *in this particular community of faith a certain kind of God has been made known to me.*

Believing in a certain kind of God is what I mean when I say that I am a Christian and not some other kind of believer—a Buddhist or Muslim, or a believer from one of the other great religious traditions. But it is not always easy to believe in such a way, to believe in such a God. In the concrete, daily conditions of my life and the lives of others, problems and tensions arise when I try to understand what such belief means. How do I go about relating belief in God to the decisions I have to make and the kind of life I have to lead? What kind of person does my belief require me to become? And what of the problems and tensions arising from my own doubt and despair or the doubt and despair of others? How do we continue to believe in a God who is present in Jesus Christ and the Holy Spirit, one who will make all things new, when we are confronted by the travail of this sad world: hatred, war, violence, injustice, poverty, and all the rest that we read about in the papers or see on our streets and on the television news? The world is full of pain, and it can often be hard to believe in God. All Christian people must deal with such questions, for they arise from the tension between our belief in a certain kind of God and the conditions of our humanity; the world we live in is far from the kingdom promised to us.

Many of us find in Anglicanism a community of faith which, we believe, provides us with a way of believing without denying that this tension of belief is real and present. We may not always be able to give clear and definite answers, and the answers we do give may not always be the best ones; but we believe that our way of dealing with the problems and questions makes it possible for us to continue to believe in the God who is present in Jesus Christ and the Holy Spirit. It is what I would call a way of believing *with* the community of faith, being sustained in belief by those with whom I share both belief and struggle—the church. The church, we believe, with all of its history of failure, is still the community of people set apart for.God. We are set apart in order to be the personal presence and witness of God in the world, the Body of Christ, a worshiping community, and a place of judgment, grace, and the hope of glory.

Those of us for whom the church is a deeply important part of our lives are certainly aware of the disparity between what we believe about God, and the church as it actually exists in history. Perhaps we are even more aware of the disparity than those outside it. We try to understand it by looking to Jesus Christ, that is, by looking at what believing in Jesus as Savior tells us about God and God's ways with us. When we look to Jesus as the truth about God and about our own lives, we believe we are shown that the holy and transcendent God comes to us in all we have to go through. God comes to us and stays with us, not just as some fleeting presence, a stranger who drops in for a call, but as someone who abides with us in all that really matters in human life: joy, love, a desire for justice, courage, and forgiveness, as well as failure, pain, suffering, and death. As Christians we believe that God is with us in the community we call *church*, the community that believes that the God who is beyond all history is, in the life of the human being Jesus, present with us in our history—our history as individuals and our history as a church.

Sometimes I would like to think that the God made known in Jesus Christ is not what God is really like. Sometimes I think I would prefer a God who sits tranquilly on a throne in heaven, far removed from human agony and pain. It can be easier to believe in a God who will just reach down from time to time and pluck me and those I love out of the mess we have got ourselves into—a *deus ex machina* of the old dramas in which God comes down in a chariot, solves all of the problems of this messy world, and then goes back to heaven to the applause of all. I can even find myself praying in such a way: "Please, God, solve all my problems; clean up the world; make everything fine, because after all you have the power to make the bad things just go away." But believing in Jesus Christ won't allow me to believe or pray in such a way—or at least not for very long. Believing in Jesus always makes me look to the God who is in the mess with me, helping me to deal with it and transforming it and me in the process, not just plucking me out of it.

Sometimes I also think I would like to belong to a church that is pure and holy, with no grubbiness, no sinners, no politics, no need for insurance policies or legal advice, and certainly not one composed of people who are in pain, who are suffering, and who have to make hard decisions about drugs, sex, abortion, assisted suicide, and shady financial deals. Parish life would be a lot easier without all those problems. When I was teaching in theological seminaries, I found that students each year would arrive full of dreams about how wonderful it would be to spend three years in prayer and study, surrounded by other holy people and far removed from the temptations of the world, the flesh, and the devil: the church the way it *ought to be*. Alas, the dreams did not last long, and the students in fact learned very quickly that they and their fellow seminarians led lives just as confused and sinful as those "in the world."

Of course, there is a difference between struggling with the confusion and sin of our lives while living in a community that believes in a God who is present with us in Jesus Christ and struggling along in a world that believes in a God who is absent and aloof. For the Christian, what makes the difference is our belief in Jesus Christ. Belief in Jesus calls us to believe that God, the eternal and holy one, is with us in death as in life, in sorrow and in joy. This is what we mean when we say that we believe that God is with us in Jesus Christ. In his life, death, and resurrection, and in his exaltation and the sending of the Spirit at Pentecost, Jesus shows us who God is; and, through his Spirit, he makes it possible for us to have faith in the God who rules this sad world and who will bring it to glory.

The creeds and the Chalcedonian Definition have been formal ways of stating this belief in Jesus Christ for many generations. They are statements about what the Christian community has believed in order to get the story right. Being able to tell the story of Jesus right, of course, involved many factors: theological writings, sermons, the instruction of new converts at baptism, the way in which the early Christians dealt with the world in which they lived, and especially worship. The early Christians believed that in worship they not only told the story of Jesus—his life, death, resurrection, and exaltation—they also entered into that story; in worship they took part in the mystery of redemption made possible by the life of Jesus. So the Incarnation was not simply a verbal formula that someone thought up; it was first and foremost the doctrine which expressed in words the new life which they were given in Christ.

In Anglicanism, as it has developed historically, much the same thing has been true. The Incarnation of God in Christ has become for us something more than a truth or doctrine about Jesus. It has become for us an expression of our *way of believing*—our way of believing in God and what our believing in God says about us. Belief in the Incarnation is a matter of *identity* for Anglicans and is important to the way we understand the church and the way we interpret the Bible. For that reason Anglicans have always looked to the decisions of the ecumenical councils and the difficult doctrinal statements they developed for help in interpreting the Bible and for upholding the doctrines of Trinity and Incarnation.

But for Anglicans the Incarnation is also a way of believing through what we do in worship. The worship of God, as it becomes the deep life of heart and mind, is to be *in Christ:* in his humanity, his oneness with us as human beings, we offer ourselves to the God with whom Jesus is one in his divinity. Just as through its worship the church of the first centuries came to believe in "God with us," that is, God present in Jesus Christ, so too for many Anglicans worship is the way in which we come to believe in the God present in Jesus Christ. What, then, is this act which is so central to Christian belief in Jesus Christ and so fundamental also for us who are Anglicans? This question brings us to the topic of Anglicans at worship.

Chapter 6

Anglican Worship

Worship arises out of a fundamental characteristic of what it is to be human: our need to deal with the question of meaning. As far as we know human beings are unique among the sensate animals of this world in our search for meaning. We ponder the "Why?" questions that begin early in childhood—Why do I have to go to bed now?—and continue to the end of life—Why does the person I love have to suffer so? Why do I have to die? Philosophers, theologians, and scientists have their own "Why?" questions: Why is there something rather than nothing? Why do things happen the way they do?

We all know, too, that the answers we give to our "Why?" questions are not very satisfactory. The child who is told that she has to go to bed now "because I say so" is probably no more content with the answer than the scientist seeking to understand the origins of the universe, or the person watching a loved one die from cancer. The answers we give just don't fit the questions we ask because ultimate questions push us beyond the explanations we can usually give for the ordinary questions of our lives. We can understand many things in our world, but certain ultimate questions about life and death, suffering, joy, and love defy our ordinary explanations. They push us beyond to something else.

Some people would say that since we cannot answer such ultimate questions we are better off not asking them. People of faith, however, believe that such questions demand another response, one that calls us beyond our ordinary way of dealing with questions to respond through faith, hope, trust, and love. I like to think of this "calling beyond" as the courage to worship: to offer myself in praise and thanksgiving and to know myself in the presence of God. The courage to worship is not an act of resignation or one that denies or rejects what my mind can tell me. It is, rather, an act that opens me to new possibilities and understandings, showing me that my knowledge and explanations do not exhaust reality and that there is always more to my life and my world than I can think or explain or even imagine. The courage to worship puts me and my experience into a larger context. Let me give an example of how I think worship works for us.

One of the ways we try to deal with the ultimate questions we cannot answer is to tell stories. The ancient myths of creation, savior gods, the Fates of Greek mythology, and accounts of heaven and hell are such stories. Families, friends, and communities also tell stories—how they began, how they faced trials and tribulations, how they have rejoiced in victories won. The stories connect us to our history; they enable us to take part in a drama bigger than ourselves and to understand ourselves as part of a larger story about hope and redemption, beginnings and endings. They do not answer the ultimate questions, but they place them in a context which gives meaning to our individual experience.

The Hebrew people tell such a story in recounting their Exodus from Egypt into the Promised Land. In this event, the story says, is the meaning of your life as a people with God; no matter what happens, here is the meaning of everything else that may happen, because here you see what God is doing and how your God is faithful. Throughout centuries of persecution and wandering, Jews have retold this story in order to say who they are, to give them an identity as a people, and to rekindle their courage to go on. Survivors of the Holocaust tell of the importance for them of recalling and remembering the story of the Exodus in the concentration camps. For some, it enabled them to have the courage to continue to believe and survive.

We Christians also tell the story of our Exodus—the story of the death and resurrection of Jesus, who is, we believe, God with us in our human history. In this event, our story says, God acts in Jesus Christ to save, to bring us from death to life. Liturgical worship calls us into the death and resurrection of Jesus; it makes his story our story, and so it is the meaning of all that happens to us as Christian people.

In the Episcopal Church we tell the story of our Exodus in the services of baptism and eucharist. The sacrament of baptism is our incorporation into the story of God's act of redemption in Jesus Christ. In it we become part of the story. When a child or adult is to be baptized, the officiant says the following prayer over the water and through the prayer she or he tells the Christian story:

> We thank you, Almighty God, for the gift of water. Over it the Holy Spirit moved in the beginning of creation. Through it you led the children of Israel out of their bondage in Egypt into the land of promise. In it your Son Jesus received the baptism of John and was anointed by the Holy Spirit as the Messiah, the Christ,

to lead us, through his death and resurrection, from the bondage of sin into everlasting life. (BCP 306)

In the prayers of the eucharist we tell the story of salvation once again:

Father, you loved the world so much that in the fullness of time you sent your only Son to be our Savior. Incarnate by the Holy Spirit, born of the Virgin Mary, he lived as one of us, yet without sin. To the poor he proclaimed the good news of salvation; to prisoners, freedom; to the sorrowful, joy. To fulfill your purpose he gave himself up to death; and, rising from the grave, destroyed death, and made the whole creation new. And that we might live no longer for ourselves, but for him who died and rose for us, he sent the Holy Spirit, his own first gift for those who believe, to complete his work in the world, and to bring to fulfillment the sanctification of all. (BCP 374)

Both liturgies tell the story and also act it out: the person is immersed in the water, and we receive the blessed bread and wine of the eucharist as the sign of the crucified and risen Christ present among us.

In other words, we not only tell stories; we also act out what we are trying to say. In our ordinary human relationships we have what we call ritual actions that express a meaning we cannot express in words—touching and holding another person, making love, sharing a meal together, giving a gift, making a gesture of hospitality and welcome, perhaps even just sending a birthday card. They are all very ordinary human actions. So too are baptism and eucharist—washing in water and eating a meal together. But in worship those ordinary human actions are

transformed; they become acts through which we ourselves live into the story we have told.

Here then is what I mean by the courage to worship.
The liturgy takes our personal and individual prayers, our
stumbling words of petition for ourselves and others, and
our sometimes half-hearted words of thanksgiving or confession, and transforms them all into God's Word to us and
to the world in which we live. The problems are not solved:
people still die of cancer, we don't always get what we
want, and we are still caught up in our own sins and
failures, but God's Word of faithfulness, Jesus Christ, is
present. The courage to worship is to believe in the final
victory of God, not as "pie in the sky by and by," but as
that which gives meaning to an otherwise tragic and
shattered world.

The courage to worship goes even further. It *enables* us
to go on with something more than resignation to our fate:
we can offer praise and give thanks to God even in death.
That is what we proclaim when in baptism and eucharist
we tell the story of the death and resurrection of Jesus: we
can give thanks for life emerging from death. Heaven
knows, it is not easy to do that, and much of the time we
certainly fail. But in worship we are able to remember who
we are, we are able to hear and believe in God's victory. Our
communion with one another is a participation now for
those of us who believe and a sign to those who do not yet
believe of God's promise in Jesus Christ.

This sense of being a sacramental community, one
which tells the story of Jesus and calls us to enter into that
story through worship, is one of the gifts of the Catholic
Revival in Anglicanism. The Catholic Revival enabled us to
regain our heritage as a sacramental community because
it saw clearly that the church is grounded in the Incarnation of God in Christ. I think it would be true to say that

we in the Episcopal Church are becoming better able to understand ourselves as a sacramental and incarnational community through our worship because of the 1979 *Book of Common Prayer*. The 1979 Prayer Book has enabled us to come to a greater awareness of the implications of believing in Jesus Christ as the heart of the church. Its services of worship have opened the way for us to understand more deeply that the Incarnation expresses our belief about the relationship between God and our humanity, and that the sacramental life is the living out of that relationship in the church and in the world.

The baptismal service in the 1979 Prayer Book is a good example of this change in the way we live out our faith. In the Episcopal Church those who are committing themselves to Christ at their baptism, and those who are renewing their commitment, together take part in the Baptismal Covenant, which is usually affirmed four times a year at public worship. The Baptismal Covenant expresses our common and fundamental faith as Christian people—what makes us Christians, not just Episcopalians. We are baptized into Christ, not, as people sometimes say, into the Episcopal Church.

The Baptismal Covenant includes the affirmation of the Apostles' Creed (the church's earliest confession of Christian belief), as well as various promises reflecting the consequences of our belief. We promise to continue in the apostles' teaching and fellowship; to be faithful in worship and prayer; to resist evil and to repent when we fail; to proclaim by word and example the gospel; to seek and to serve Christ in all persons; and to strive for justice and peace and to respect the dignity of every human being. These baptismal promises in the 1979 Prayer Book are enabling Episcopalians to struggle with new issues—the current conflicts about sexual morality, economic justice, and racism within society, for example—which have emerged for Christian people in the world in which they live and in which they believe the Incarnate Christ is present and active.

As the sacrament of baptism speaks of our incorporation into the community of God's people, so the eucharist is the sign of our continuing participation in God's work of salvation for all humankind—both those who believe and those who do not yet believe. Baptism and eucharist make the Incarnation concrete in our lives: Jesus Christ is not just someone in the past, a historical figure we remember, whom we read about in a book or hear about from others; he is God present with us now. When, through our worship, we enter into the story of his human life with us, he opens the way to God. What is this service of worship—the Holy Eucharist—which is so central to the life of Anglicans?

My years of worshiping in the Episcopal Church have shown me that in worship I participate in and have communion with God through the story of Jesus, who is God with us. My journey as an Anglican Christian has led me to explore more deeply *how* the Incarnation is at the center of our life and how the worship of the Episcopal Church can help us believe that this is so.

The parish church in which I began to learn the meaning of the Incarnation and its relation to worship enabled me to learn something which was quite new for me about *believing in God*. I had always believed that God existed, and I had, as all good children did in those days, accepted God's authority in my life, just as I had accepted the authority of my parents and teachers in school. But the God in whom I had believed was an austere male figure "up there" who made the rules and regulations which governed my life. "He" was not someone with whom I had any personal contact.

Discovering worship in that particular parish opened a new world for me because I began to have a sense that God was present in my life. God was someone who worried about me in a different way than my parents worried about me. God was one who could listen to things which I could not tell my parents and friends or anyone else. Worshiping in the eucharist was the means through which I came to believe *in* God, not just believe things *about* God.

Gradually, also, as I worshiped God through the eucharist and received Holy Communion, I began to pray for myself, and even occasionally for others, in a much more personal and serious manner. I began to pray to someone whom I was coming to know, not just someone I had heard about. The "bless mommy, bless daddy" prayers of my childhood took on new meaning as I began to have a deeper sense of the presence of God in my life and in the lives of those I loved. My prayers for myself and others were incorporated into a larger act of offering—offering which was both praying for myself and others, as well as giving thanks. For that is what eucharist is: holding others in Christ and giving thanks to God.

Also, I began to have a sense of sin and failure that went beyond the naughtiness of childhood. I began to see that sin was not simply breaking a rule or a law, doing something my parents had told me not to do or my peers thought was wrong. Confessing my sins in the context of worship helped me to see that sin involved the breaking of a relationship; it was a failure in love. Consequently, I slowly came to see that forgiveness was something more than being patted on the head and told that all was well, or being approved of by those who mattered. Forgiveness asked something of me, and I began to learn the meaning of repentance.

In a novel that was popular some years ago, one of the characters says, in effect, "Love means never having to say you're sorry." I am not sure what the character in the novel meant; perhaps she did not know herself. But through the eucharist, I learned that love, both of God and neighbor, *does* require saying you are sorry; it means the deep sorrow of knowing that you have broken a relationship through your sin. Repentance is not beating oneself on the head; it is acknowledging a failure of love, a failure to give and receive. Through worship I was being shown how my sin and my failure to love could be taken up into the deeper love of God in Christ. I was being shown something of the responsibility of saying "I'm sorry" and of forgiveness as the acceptance of responsibility for personal failure, an acceptance made possible because one is loved.

How I would have talked about all these matters then, I do not know; I can only talk about them now with the hindsight and the vocabulary that has come with years. I can certainly say, however, that what began in the eucharist for me as a young man has remained with me over the years. As I have gone on worshiping God in a community of Christians gathered for the eucharist, I believe I have grown in the "knowledge and love of God," so that the doctrines I learned about God through the church's teaching and through my own reading and study began to make sense. For me, as I know has been true for many others, worshiping God in the eucharist has led to both believing and understanding.

I also discovered something else, although it took longer for me to appreciate it and to find the words to express it. I learned that in worship I was not just receiving something from God; I was also offering or giving something of myself to God in Jesus Christ. This was a major step in discovering a truth which has become increasingly important to me as I have gone on in my journey with God: that who I am—all of my complex emotions and desires, and my mind with all of its doubts, conflicts, hopes, and fears—has something to do with God. I can still remember the impact it made upon me to realize that the money that I gave and the bread and the wine brought forward for the eucharist were an offering of myself, *me*, to God. I was, so to speak, there on the altar being transformed in the eucharistic prayer. To paraphrase a saying of Augustine of Hippo, I began to see that in what I offered, I was myself being offered. The eucharistic prayer of the 1928 *Book of Common Prayer* we used then (and still use in Rite I liturgies) taught me much about God and myself:

> And here we offer and present unto thee, O Lord, our selves, our souls and bodies, to be a reasonable, holy, and living sacrifice unto thee; humbly beseeching thee that we, and all others who shall be partakers of this Holy Communion, may worthily receive the most precious Body and Blood of thy Son Jesus Christ, be filled with thy grace and heavenly benediction, and made one body with him, that he may dwell in us, and we in him. (BCP 336)

To *present, partake, receive,* and *be made one body:* this was eucharistic worship. It led me to see that I not only had to pay attention to God; I also had to pay attention to myself. For a young man, as I then was, paying attention to yourself is not especially difficult, but paying attention to yourself while paying attention to God requires considerable work.

So, the eucharist went hand in hand with my emotional and intellectual development. What happened on Sunday

morning in the eucharist and what happened during the
week at school, in relationships with friends and family,
and in the gradual and sometimes painful discovery of
myself happened to the same person. I often did my best to
keep God and myself separate—not letting the right hand
know what the left hand was doing, as we say. But the
eucharist always pulled me on and made me realize that
the real person I was and was struggling to become was
the person who was in relationship to God: *I* was the person
whom God loved and wanted, not someone else smarter,
more holy and pure, or more obedient and less driven by
"pride, vanity, and self-conceit," but *me*.

God and me; God and all other human beings like me;
offering and being offered in Christ: this is to believe in the
Incarnation. It is what I have learned in heart and mind as
the eucharist of offering and being offered has become the
basic structure for my belief and practice as a Christian.

As a consequence of growing into the eucharist, worship
has made it possible for me to believe in God as one whom
I can love, as well as one whom I can know intellectually.
There is a considerable difference between knowing and
loving, although ultimately the two must become one. But
for someone like myself, who tends to intellectualize belief,
it has been important for me to be shown over and over
again that belief *in* God means to know what we love and
love what we know, as Augustine wrote about his own
growth into God. Eucharistic worship shows me the necessity of finding the unity of both. By being called into
personal relationship with the holy and eternal God, I have
been shown that belief *in* God is more than believing certain
propositions *about* God and more than I am able to imagine
about God. As the gospel of John puts it, "And the Word
became flesh and lived among us, and we have seen his
glory, the glory as of a father's only son, full of grace and

truth" (John 1:14). Try as I might—and sometimes I have tried very hard indeed—I cannot intellectualize away Jesus of Nazareth. He is someone whom I must continually seek to know as the Word of the eternal God and "in the flesh."

Through all this growing up, therefore, eucharistic worship made it possible for me to come to a greater knowledge and understanding of myself. It gave me the courage to believe in myself as well as the courage to offer myself to God, to know myself in communion with God through Christ, in other words. The word "courage" is not inappropriate here. It takes courage to offer yourself to God—for God is a living fire, a burning bush—but in the Christ of the eucharist I learned that I *could* offer myself because Christ himself as a human being like me had offered himself. I did not have to hide myself from God, like Adam and Eve in the garden, nor did I have to despair because of who I was. I could have the courage to offer myself because the God who comes to us in Christ would receive me and was eager to enter into communion with me—"just as I am, without one plea, but that thy blood was shed for me," as the old hymn puts it.

These two dimensions of the eucharist—what it means to believe *in* God and to have the courage to offer myself *to* God—were important to me as a young man; they became increasingly important to me as an adult. I would say now that I was learning then what it is to engage in a form of worship which arises out of—finds its source in—the Incarnation of God in Christ, namely, that God is personally with us in all that happens to us.

I believe that what has happened to me in my own journey with God from adolescence to adulthood in the Episcopal Church has happened and continues to happen for many others who "come home" or find a home in this community of believers. I began by being attracted to the ritual of worship—"the smells and bells" as we used to say. As I have gone on I have found much more. I have found the sacramental life of worship in which my personal life has been shaped by entering into the Christian story and having God transform my life. The sacramental life of worship is making concrete in the life of believers what the Definition of the Council of Chalcedon sought to express in words about the Incarnation: in Jesus, who is one with us and one with God, we are transformed.

Chapter 7

Identity and Diversity

In the last several chapters we have been looking at the origins, mission, beliefs, and worship of Anglicanism and the Episcopal Church. I believe (though others might interpret our history quite differently) that our history and foundations demonstrate a pattern of continuity and change—continuity with the tradition of the gospel we have received in Christ and, at the same time, a willingness to interpret and understand that gospel as changing situations might require. And I have suggested further that the way in which we have understood and believed in the Incarnation has made this pattern possible for us; the Incarnation has centered us as a worshiping and sacramental community.

For me, as someone who has spent all of his formative years in this sacramental and worshiping community, the Episcopal Church has a clear identity—I know what the Episcopal Church is for me because it has been my family. I have lived with it, prayed with it, and struggled with it. However, those who have come to this church more recently and long-time Episcopalians who see their church wobbling between one position and another, tolerating a great deal of diversity, might very well say, "It's fine to be a sacramental and worshiping community, but what does the Episcopal Church *stand* for? What gives it an identity and an authority? What holds it together?" For many it now seems that the Episcopal Church is suffering from an identity crisis.

I cannot hope to answer such questions definitively, because others have their own perspective on the Episcopal Church—that they do is part of what makes us all Episcopalians. But I do hope in this chapter to make some suggestions about how those questions might be approached. In other words, I want to explore what gives the Episcopal Church an identity and authority even while we live with great diversity. I believe the key lies once again in the Incarnation.

Christians have always been concerned with the doctrine of Christ—and not simply because of its opportunities for theological quibbling. Who Jesus was, and is, affects the ordinary life and belief of Christian people—how we pray and worship, what we believe about the sacraments, how we act in the world, what kind of church we are a part of, and how that church carries out its mission. In working through these questions and controversies of belief and practice the early church came to understand one thing quite clearly, and it was central to their theological debates: the identity, unity, and ultimate mission of the church was to be found only in the Incarnate Christ. For them Jesus Christ was God's personal and saving presence in the church, guiding and directing it through the events, controversies, and crises with which it had to deal. In other words, they believed that the Incarnation is the *active* center around which everything else moves—doctrine, church government, patterns of worship and ministry, and the moral and spiritual life of Christian people. Without that center nothing else matters; it is what makes the church the church.

This early church of the patristic period, when all the controversies over the Incarnation were taking place, was certainly an institution in the world, tangled up with the complex politics of the later Roman empire. Those politics had consequences for how the doctrine of Christ itself developed and was formulated. At the same time, however, even the most ardent polemicists of the period believed that the institution, with its structures and political concerns, must always direct members of the church beyond themselves to the God who, in Christ, is the center of the church. This belief is what led to arguments about the doctrine of the Incarnation in the first place, as I tried to show in an earlier chapter.

Although the historical parallels are certainly not exact, the Church of England at the time of the Reformation was also struggling with a confusion in matters of faith and practice. In throwing off the old authority of the pope and what the papacy represented as a source of church unity and authority, the English church found itself in considerable conflict between what it had been and what it was in the process of becoming. Likewise, the Episcopal Church after the Revolutionary War had to discover ways to maintain its continuity with the doctrine, discipline, and worship of the Church of England (and through it with the church of the Bible and the early councils), while also learning how to be a new church in a new nation. It had to discover its identity and authority as an *American* church, not simply a continuation of the church in former English colonies.

Similar tensions have arisen for all national churches in the Anglican Communion as they have freed themselves from the old British empire or the more recent American empire: how to be in continuity with all that Anglicanism represents and yet not be held captive by the Church of England or the Episcopal Church. When I was teaching in Puerto Rico I found that Anglicans there, as well as in Haiti, Central America, and other nations, struggled constantly with that problem. They owed their existence as a church to American missionaries and money, and they had to explore the question of what it meant to be an Anglican without being a *norteamericano* or gringo.

I believe that it is this tension of continuity and change at the heart of Anglicanism from its beginning that has made us look only to the Incarnate Christ as the source of our identity and authority as we have worked our way through historical changes and confusions. We have no pope, as the Roman Catholic Church has, and we have no formal confession of faith, as the churches of the Reformation have, to give us identity as Anglicans. We have the Bible, certainly, but that makes us Christians, not necessarily Anglicans. At one time we all had a *Book of Common Prayer* derived from the English prayer book, but all Anglican churches have now revised their prayer books extensively. In one sense, all Anglicans have is the Archbishop of Canterbury, and he, in the final analysis, is just another English bishop. So we have been required by our historical circumstances to look to Christ alone for our identity and authority as a church. And this may well be the witness we have to make to the one, holy, catholic, and apostolic church.

Nowhere can this reliance upon Christ be better seen than in Richard Hooker. As he sought to justify the Anglican position over against the Puritans and the Roman Catholics at the beginning of Anglican self-consciousness, Hooker refused to tie down the Church of England to one view of how the church ought to be constituted, or to one fixed formula for its belief and practice. The church, he believed, found its justification, as well as its life of sacramental worship and practice, in the Incarnation. The Incarnation meant for him that the church is at once a human and divine society, one in which authority for discipline and doctrine always derived from the grace of God in Christ and not from the claim of human certainty. Hooker returned over and over again to the incarnational theme of divine action and human response, God and human history, as the foundation and the hope of the church's existence, just as he saw the sacraments that derived from the Incarnate Christ as the means for our unity with God.

This theme has been repeated over and over again in Anglican thinking—taking with utmost seriousness the concerns and conflicts of the historical existence of the church, while yet believing that all the church does is centered in Christ. It returned again in the Catholic Revival as the Episcopal Church struggled with its own identity, and it shaped the new thinking of the contributors to *Lux Mundi* as they looked to Christ as the Light of the world, the Truth of God made known in history.

Archbishop Michael Ramsey summed up this recurring theme when he said of Anglicanism that

> its credentials are its incompleteness, with the tension and travail in its soul. It is clumsy and untidy, it baffles neatness and logic. For it is sent not to commend itself as "the best type of Christianity," but by its very brokenness to point to the universal Church wherein all have died.[1]

Believing that the Incarnate Christ is the only source for the identity and authority of the church has stood us in good stead through many of the crises and conflicts we have continued to face in the twentieth century. It has enabled us to be a church that can incorporate new forms of thought and new discoveries into our understanding of the Christian tradition of belief and practice. It is this ability that gives Anglicanism its sense of identity. We are a community of belief and practice that can live with change, and the diversity that results from change, with a certain degree of spiritual confidence or courage: a courage to believe in the face of conflict and change is, one might say, a quality of Anglican identity.

We have been able to accept contemporary biblical criticism, for example, because we can appreciate the authority of scripture within the context of the Incarnate Christ: the Bible is not the only or last word of God to us. Certainly it is, as Hooker said, "an oracle of God," but it is also a historical book, one written by fallible human beings. We can believe that by the guiding of the Holy Spirit its writers were led to witness authentically to the revelation of God in Christ, but most Anglican biblical scholars and theologians, as well as most ordinary Episcopalians, would agree that it always needs to be interpreted and understood within the church itself—in the light of Christ.

Biblical scholars in the Episcopal Church such as Reginald Fuller, Frederick Borsch, and William Countryman have helped Episcopalians to understand the authority of the Bible in the context of the larger authority of Christ who still speaks to the church through the Holy Spirit. Frederick Borsch speaks of Anglicanism's tolerance,

> enabling Anglican Christians to use the Bible both seriously and with the responsible freedom it inspires....As central and essential as the Bible is, it is not an absolute authority but points the Church instead to the discernment of the Spirit of God working within the community.[2]

Another area in which our sense of identity and authority arises from our reliance upon the Incarnate Christ is our
willingness to allow philosophy, science, and the arts to
inform and even interpret our belief. John Macquarrie, one
of the major Anglican contributors to systematic theology
in this century, makes use of the philosophy of Martin
Heidegger to illuminate Christian belief. Heidegger did not
consider himself a Christian, but he did think deeply about
the issues of human existence in our disordered world—and
because he was an outsider, he was able to point to the
tragic dimensions of the loss of faith.

In *Principles of Christian Theology*, Macquarrie describes
how such philosophical analysis, even when it is not explicitly Christian, can serve as a means for articulating and
elucidating Christian truth when, "like theologians of the
past, we can avail ourselves of such current philosophical
work as will best serve to express the faith in terms that
communicate with the secular culture of our time." In such
a context Macquarrie states his own allegiance to the
Anglican *via media* as one way of relating theology to "the
polarities of human existence itself." Christ, in other words,
as the Incarnate Word of God, is the "new and decisive
revelation of an activity" which has always been present in
creation itself—even among the philosophers.[3]

The openness of Anglicanism to artistic expression is
well-known. We have encouraged musicians, painters, and
writers to bring their work to the church, even when it has
not been explicitly Christian, and we have learned much
from them about the Incarnate Christ. When I was in
Puerto Rico, I had personal contact with one example of
this openness to artistic expression. When "primitive"
painters in Haiti began to develop a significant school of
native painting, they found it hard to gain any kind of
acceptance or recognition—now, of course, they are highly

regarded. The Episcopal Bishop of Haiti, who took an interest in their work, turned his cathedral over to them. They transformed the walls with profound and deeply moving paintings of biblical stories in the context of peasant life in Haiti. They were able to "tell the story of Jesus" in fresh and vibrant ways. Those who had criticized the bishop for welcoming "pagans" were forced to change their minds: the Incarnate Christ, working through "outsiders," had transformed what the critics had thought to be foreign to Christ.

These are only examples of what the Incarnation has meant to Anglicanism. They show, however, ways in which what we have believed about the unity of the divine and human, God and humanity, in Christ has led us to an Anglican identity. For Anglicans the church mediates the truth of the transcendent God to human beings; it mediates the truth of God's revelation in and through its own fragility and incompleteness. But it also brings the truth about our humanity to God for reconciliation and transformation in Christ. Sinners in need of redemption we certainly are, but we are all also capable of much good. The church, as the Incarnation shows us, can be a sign of God's presence to us and our presence to God.

As a community which worships, hears, and discerns the truth made known to us in Christ, we also need to express what we believe that truth to be. Anglicans do this in various ways, chiefly through our doctrines and our forms of worship. For the Episcopal Church and for the other churches of the Anglican Communion this body of belief and practice as it has developed over the centuries has its fullest and most authoritative expression in the *Book of*

Common Prayer. The prayer books of the Anglican Communion differ from church to church, but they all draw
together the belief expressed in Holy Scripture and the
theological and moral traditions of the church as Anglicans
have received and understood them. Consequently, it is to
the *Book of Common Prayer* that we turn when we want to
say, "This is the Anglican way of believing; this is what we
mean when we say that we believe in God." All those who
are ordained and who have authority to teach in Anglican
churches and the Episcopal Church must promise to conform to the teaching expressed in the *Book of Common
Prayer.*

Thus the *Book of Common Prayer* is something of a
hermeneutical key for Anglicanism. "Hermeneutics" is a
very current theological term which simply means, in this
context, a way of interpreting biblical material—or the lens
through which we read it. Any literary text or, for that
matter, any artistic creation or historical event or some
occurrence in our own lives needs to be interpreted and
understood, incorporated within a larger scheme of other
events and beliefs. We can interpret texts or events through
political, theological, psychological, or economic lenses or
categories. Whatever hermeneutical key we use does not
exhaust all the possibilities for understanding the material,
but it does provide us with one way of interpreting it.

This is how the *Book of Common Prayer* functions for
Anglicans: we interpret and understand the Bible and the
doctrinal and moral tradition of the church through the
way we worship and pray together as a community of the
baptized. So, when we say, "If you want to know what we
Episcopalians believe, come and worship with us," we are
saying that our way of worshiping expresses our way of
believing. This is what we mean by *lex orandi, lex cre-*

dendi—the rule of praying is the rule of believing. Liturgical scholar Leonel L. Mitchell has put it well:

> In a real sense...we Episcopalians are liturgical theologians. We read our theology out of the *Book of Common Prayer* and the manner in which we celebrate its services. Formally, the theology of the liturgy is called primary theology, or *theologia prima*. Theology is "God-talk," and primary theology is the language we use when we talk *with* God, not simply the words we speak, but the entire liturgical act....The primary nature of the language of worship is real and important. For example, it is not necessary for every Christian to understand the doctrine of the Trinity as it is spelled out in the Athanasian Creed.[4] However, it is necessary for every Christian to offer prayer and praise to the Father and Creator of all through Jesus Christ in the fellowship of the Holy Spirit, for such is at the heart of our faith.[5]

Because our way of worshiping and praying interprets our way of believing, we in the Episcopal Church and Anglican churches elsewhere have revised the *Book of Common Prayer* from time to time, not only to make the language more intelligible (for words do change in meaning), but also to give expression to what we believe about God and salvation in Christ in a different time and place. The current prayer book of the Episcopal Church, for example, has incorporated many prayers and practices from the early church, clarifying our continuity with traditions that predate the theological controversies of the Reformation or the liturgical practices of other times.

Two very important examples of such changes concern baptism and the eucharist. The 1979 *Book of Common Prayer* makes it clear that baptism is a public act of incorporation into the community of faith. We baptize in the presence of the whole congregation gathered on Sunday morning, not in a private service for immediate family and friends, as was done for many years in the Episcopal Church. Similarly, in the 1979 Prayer Book the Holy Eucharist is the normative act of worship for the church because it is our recollection in this present time of the event that makes us Christians: the death and resurrection of Jesus Christ. Through the action of recalling that event in the eucharist, we who are baptized into Christ enter into his work of salvation.

Both of these changes express our renewal. They are a return to the sacramental theology of the early Christian community. It was, in fact, the Catholic Revival, with its retrieval of the sacramental theology of Richard Hooker, that made it possible for us to recover this dimension of our heritage as Anglicans, namely, that the sacraments of baptism and eucharist are the acts whereby we are joined to the Incarnate Christ, through whom we participate in the divine life of the trinitarian God.

These sacramental acts, more than any official teaching which the Episcopal Church may put forth, express our belief as Christian people. They are the actions through which we proclaim our faith in the one who is God's presence with us; they are the actions through which we tell the story of God in Christ. Whatever teaching or doctrines we may hold are subsequent to them. As another Anglican liturgical theologian, Louis Weil, has noted:

> Authentic liturgical worship draws all that is human into its frame of reference....Liturgical rites are not ceremonial clothing for doctrinal teaching. Rather than *teaching* the faith, in the usual sense of that word, the liturgy *celebrates* the faith. It lifts it up through words and signs in a corporate experience which expresses the

faith which has summoned the people to gather. Yet it also nourishes that faith, and sends the people forth to live it in their daily lives.[6]

Of course, making a common declaration of faith and acting it out in baptism does not always guarantee that everyone will agree about what we have declared and done. We still have to deal with ourselves as human beings who disagree and who may not be lifted up by a common faith and practice.

And we Episcopalians do disagree about many things. The Episcopal Church has been called the "roomiest" church in Christendom because we are very tolerant of doctrinal differences and diversity in the practice of the Christian life. Sometimes our roominess leads to considerable confusion and, even worse, to blandness or incoherence. Those from other churches who are engaged in ecumenical conversations with us frequently deplore our lack of a clear authority in matters of belief and practice. When asked what our authority is, we will often appeal, vaguely, to "catholic tradition," to our liturgy, or to the "three-legged stool" of scripture, tradition, and reason, without a clear idea of what those three legs are and how they can be used. In our history we have often adapted too easily to "the modern mind," or we have failed to appreciate the enormity of the failures of contemporary culture and human sinfulness.

There are also people within the Episcopal Church who despair of our lack of a clear and official teaching authority. Some would argue that we ought to adhere more closely to the Thirty-Nine Articles of Religion or produce a confessional statement. When bishops have questioned basic beliefs, such as the virgin birth or the resurrection, or have ordained women or homosexual persons, cries go up and threats of heresy trials are made. Roominess can be messy and uncomfortable.

How then are we to live out the faith that unites us and gives us our identity? I believe we must have the willingness, even the courage to live with a certain amount of ambiguity in matters of belief and practice. Such a stance is not easy to take, and some will find the Episcopal Church frustrating and, in the end, will not be nourished by it. However, as one who has lived with the Episcopal Church for a long time and who has found it deeply nourishing, such a willingness to live with ambiguity and to have the courage to believe deeply even while not being absolutely certain is a journey of faith in the Incarnate Christ. Let me explain what I mean.

I have found (and I believe I am not alone in this discovery) that one of the gifts of growing up from brash adolescence to, we hope, more mature adulthood is that we sometimes learn the grace to live with questions that cannot be answered with certainty. We come to realize the tentativeness of many of the decisions we have to make, and we are somewhat less inclined to assert the absolute difference between true and false, good and bad. I have certainly learned, in my history with God, the church, other people, and myself, that my decisions are not always right and my judgments are not always true. I have known myself to be wrong on too many occasions to believe that I am always right.

Even about some of my most deeply held beliefs I have learned that ambiguity, doubt, and questioning are part of my faith in God. When I began teaching in theological seminaries, I came to understand that one of my first responsibilities as a teacher of theology was to admit to my own doubts and difficulties with Christian belief and practice. Students in theological seminaries especially need to hear that the struggle with belief is a necessary part of being led into a deeper faith in God. Clergy oftentimes think that they are never allowed to doubt or to have difficulties with vocation or problems in their personal lives because it would threaten the faith of the laity. Such thinking, in addition to being patronizing, is simply naive. The people of God gather for eucharist not because they trust in the belief of the clergy, but because they believe in God.

And for most of us, faith in God means not knowing all the answers to all the hard questions. It is having the courage to believe in the God of Jesus Christ and the courage to trust what God is doing with us in life as well as in death. The author of the letter to the Hebrews put it well: "Now faith is the assurance of things hoped for, the conviction of things not seen" (Hebrews 11:1). Faith, one might say, is having the courage to believe even in the midst of all the ambiguity and doubt that life involves, just as worship is having the courage to offer God praise and thanksgiving even in the midst of human pain and desolation.

The church—in its largest, catholic sense of the whole people of God—lives with such ambiguity as well, even when some parts of it might claim otherwise. And so it needs always to be recalled to its center in the mystery of God in Christ. In its long history with God the church accumulates a lot of underbrush which occasionally needs to be cleaned out. Like most churches, the Episcopal Church can become too sure of itself and of its beliefs and practices, and it can become lazy and arrogant with the truth. And yet this need for purification too is part of our identity and calling.

In dealing with the difficult questions which now face us, we Episcopalians need to recall our history and continue to ask ourselves what it means to be a church that has found its way through the complexities of belief and practice by its trust in the Incarnate Lord and the guidance of the Holy Spirit. What such belief has meant and must continue to mean is that we believe in the God who is with us in the ambiguities, difficulties, and pains of our time and who can transform them and us into a greater glory—that is what Incarnation is all about.

In the parish where I first began to learn to believe *in* God I became very attached to the second-century hymn we sing at the eucharist:

> Father, we thank thee who hast planted
>   thy holy Name within our hearts.
> Knowledge and faith and life immortal
>   Jesus thy Son to us imparts.
> Thou, Lord, didst make all for thy pleasure,
>   didst give us food for all our days,
> giving in Christ the Bread eternal;
>   thine is the power, be thine the praise.
>
> Watch o'er thy Church O Lord, in mercy,
>   save it from evil, guard it still,
> perfect it in thy love, unite it,
>   cleansed and conformed unto thy will.
> As grain, once scattered on the hillsides,
>   was in this broken bread made one,
> so from all lands thy Church be gathered
>   into thy kingdom by thy Son.[7]

Grain scattered and broken bread made one summed up for me what was happening in the eucharist as I struggled on with my own life. But it also began to give me a vision of the church as a community which, with all of its diversity and brokenness, is called beyond itself into God.

The Episcopal Church, and Anglicanism as a whole, are not yet there, heaven knows! They provide, however, a way of believing which for many people is reasonable, one which allows us to face new questions even while being grounded in the faith and witness of a historic community of belief. More now than ever, we Anglicans need the grace and presence of God the Holy Spirit. We need to have the courage to believe and to face reality, not to run from either. In the next chapter I want to say something more about what it might mean to have the courage to believe with the church and to trust in the Lord of the church.

Chapter 8

The Church
as Sacrament

The sacramental life, arising out of belief in the incarnation of God in Christ, is deeply important for many Episcopalians in our pilgrimages with God. We have found that sacramental life in the Episcopal Church, and because of that life we remain Episcopalians despite all the conflict and ambiguity within the church. For being a member of the Episcopal Church—like any other church—is not always easy. Churches can say and do things that cause much pain; they can be "a nest of vipers" as well as "an ark of salvation." They pose to us real problems because they sometimes can make belief in God very difficult. Many committed church people find themselves saying from time to time, "Yes, I believe in God and I believe in Jesus Christ and the Holy Spirit, but I have a lot of difficulty with the church!" How can we believe that the church is the sign to others of the incarnational and sacramental life that we personally have found so important? Can we believe what the church, this very fallible and human institution, tells us about God and God's ways with human beings? How is the institutional church a sign to the world of what it means to believe in the God of Jesus Christ?

I want to suggest here that if we can think of the church as itself a sacrament, then we can better understand what it might mean to believe *with* the church, even though we often have difficulty believing *in* the church.

In our prayer book sacraments are defined as "outward and visible signs of inward and spiritual grace, given by Christ as sure and certain means by which we receive that grace" (BCP 857). The two great sacraments of the Christian tradition are baptism and eucharist. In those sacramental acts, ordinary water, bread, and wine are the outward and visible signs of God's favor toward us. Those signs are very fragile and ambiguous: water can become stagnant, wine can become sour, and bread stale. But it is in their fragility and ambiguity that they show us who God is and how God in Christ deals with us; they make God in Christ present to us in their particularity as ordinary, everyday things of this world. In baptism and eucharist they become signs or re-presentations of God's saving presence with us—both what God has done in the death and resurrection of Jesus Christ and what God will do through the Holy Spirit to bring us and the whole creation to glory. For all these reasons, they are signs of grace, of "God's favor towards us, unearned and undeserved" (BCP 858).

The prayer book liturgies of both baptism and eucharist make clear that it is not in the *strength* of the signs—water, bread, and wine—that God is present, but rather that the Spirit of God takes the signs and makes them holy and powerful. The Holy Spirit sanctifies the water of baptism in order that our sins may be forgiven and that we may be born again and live in the risen life of Jesus Christ (BCP 307). The same Spirit sanctifies the bread and wine of the eucharist in order that they may be for us the Body and Blood of Jesus Christ, "the holy food and drink of new and unending life in him" (BCP 363). Through the sanctification of the Spirit weakness becomes strength, and we, frail human beings, share in the life of God.

I want to suggest that just as the outward and visible signs of water, bread, and wine are ordinary, fragile, and ambiguous signs of God's presence with us, so too the church, comprised as it is of ordinary, fragile, and ambiguous human beings, is the outward and visible sign of God's presence with us. To put it another way: what we say and do as a church is both a sign of our ordinariness, fragility, and ambiguity *and* a sign of God's saving presence among us in the power of the Holy Spirit. The church itself, in other words, is the sacrament of God in Christ.

Sometimes, of course, it is difficult to believe this, just as it is sometimes difficult to believe that a splash of water, a piece of bread, and a sip of wine unite us to Christ. I believe that the church is the sign of God in Christ and I believe that bread and wine are the signs of God's presence in Christ because I believe in a certain kind of God. I believe in a God whose Spirit dwells in me and makes it possible for me to believe, and I believe in a God who gives me the courage to believe even as I know and have to accept the weakness and even the foolishness of the medium through which God's gracious presence is with me and with the church.

St. Paul had some strong things to say about the weakness of human signs:

> For God's foolishness is wiser than human wisdom, and God's weakness is stronger than human strength.... God chose what is foolish in the world to shame the wise; God chose what is weak in the world to shame the strong. God chose what is low and despised in the world, things that are not, to reduce to nothing things that are, so that no one might boast in the presence of God....I

came to you in weakness and in fear and in much
trembling. My speech and my proclamation were not
with plausible words of wisdom, but with a demonstra-
tion of the Spirit and of power, so that your faith might
rest not on human wisdom but on the power of God.
(1 Cor. 1:25–2:5)

These are words which we church people ought to ponder
from time to time—not just about our own preaching, but
also about the church itself. God uses the weak things of
this world to make known by the Spirit the wisdom of God
and our hope for glory. No church can boast before God.
To understand this is to understand the sacramentality of
the church itself as the sign of God's incarnate presence in
Jesus Christ.

Anyone who has struggled with God in prayer will, I think,
have a sense of what I mean here. For prayer too is
sacramental: it is our very human struggle in our own
spirit to allow the Spirit of God to speak to us and direct
us. We use words as well as wordless cries for help or
guidance; we ask God to show us the way to go; or we ask
God to heal or help someone we love. But our words, hopes,
and even the prayers themselves oftentimes get in the way.
We tell God what to do, and we try to justify ourselves and
our actions. We use the words of our prayers to convince
ourselves that we are right about what we have already
decided to do. We can even use the words of our prayers to
condemn others or to convince ourselves that another
person is wrong.

In other words, we spend a great deal of time in prayer
struggling with ourselves, getting in the way, shutting out

the Spirit of God. Most of the time, what we are offering in our prayers is our weakness and our need, our own fragility and the ambiguities of our own lives. And it is precisely in that struggle with ourselves and our own weakness that the Spirit of God breaks through, and we hear God rather than ourselves. Again, St. Paul:

> Likewise the Spirit helps us in our weakness; for we do not know how to pray as we ought, but that very Spirit intercedes with sighs too deep for words. And God, who searches the heart, knows what is the mind of the Spirit, because the Spirit intercedes for the saints according to the will of God. (Rom. 8:26-27)

I have learned over the years that being in the Episcopal Church is very much like praying. In our human weakness we, as a community of faith, struggle with the Spirit of God in order to learn and to be shown what the Spirit would have us be and believe. The stands we take as a church, the disciplines we impose upon ourselves and others, the customs and practices that mean so much to us, are not always the right ones. In fact, they can sometimes be quite wrong—the long history of our justification of slavery, for example, or the oppression of women, or our current failure, as some are arguing, to deal honestly with human sexuality. In these and other matters we have only begun to see our failures and weaknesses, even our foolishness, as Paul says. And we shall continue to struggle with the Spirit as we seek to know God's will about the very complex issues which lie ahead.

So, we pray that God will guide the church into truth. We pray that God will, by the Spirit, grant us "to have a right judgment in all things" (BCP 227), and that the church of God may be "filled with truth and love, and be found without fault at the day of your coming" (BCP 389). Such prayers for the church should not be merely lip-service; they should express what we believe about the church as a people who need the presence of God in order to learn God's will even as we debate, argue, disagree, sometimes even condemn one another, and face the real possibility of breaking our communion. All of this struggle is part of the history of the Episcopal Church. It is the process through which, as Paul says, the Spirit prays with us, intercedes for us. We human beings who struggle with the Spirit of God are nonetheless the people of God—a stubborn, stiff-necked people, as Moses said of the people of Israel. And, like the people of Israel, we always need to be called back to our God.

It is, indeed, in the process of our struggle with the Spirit that the church becomes a sign to the world of God's presence in the Incarnate Christ. We are a sign, not in our strength, but in our weakness, because God's strength is greater than our weakness. This is the sense in which we can say not only that we believe *with* the church, but also (as we say in the Creed of Nicea) that we believe *in* the church—not the Episcopal Church, but the one, holy, catholic, and apostolic church, the Body of Christ spread throughout the world and one with the saints in glory. The substance of Christian faith is that God is faithful to the church even when we who are Episcopalians may not be.

And yet, at exactly that point of our struggle with the Spirit and even in the midst of our unfaithfulness, this worldly institution that we call the Episcopal Church can direct us beyond itself to the truth and faithfulness of God. When we say in the creeds that we believe in the one, holy, catholic, and apostolic church or when we use the biblical imagery of the church as the Body of Christ or as the sign of the reign of God, we are saying that even this fragment that we call the Episcopal Church lives in the cross and resurrection of Jesus and in the sending of the Holy Spirit. No church is sufficient unto itself. If it were, it would live only in its own death, disobedience, and faithlessness—what the cross without the resurrection tells us about our human lives and institutions. The one, holy, catholic, and apostolic church, the communion of the saints, lives in the victory of God in Christ. God's victory is the reality of which this fragile institution is a sign, a sign in which one thing is seen, but in which a greater reality is believed. Many of the people who saw Jesus saw only a poor Jewish teacher and wonder-worker; those who believed in him finally came to see in him the presence of God in their lives.

So too it can be with the community of belief that we call the Episcopal Church and in which we struggle. It is the visible sign and expression of our hope for unity with God and with one another, the communion of saints. It is also, we believe, the means—fragile and weak though it may be—which God uses in order to fulfill that hope in us and in all created things. Thus, as we also say of water, bread, and wine, the church is a means of grace, God's pledge that our hope will be fulfilled.

Such a way of thinking affirms the truth about God that is at the heart of Christian belief: God is beyond all human understanding, "immortal, invisible, God only wise, in light inaccessible, hid from our eyes," as the hymn puts it, and also Emmanuel, God with us. The church's doctrine, discipline, and patterns of worship all point and direct us to a final truth which is God, but they do so in the words, images, and actions of human beings. We human beings can, we believe, be guided by the Spirit of God into all truth, but we can also refuse to be guided and so we can badly err and distort the truth about God. God, the truth or reality in whom we believe, is deeper and richer than any of our beliefs about God. And yet, because we believe in God, we seek to express that truth as best we can in those words, images, and actions which we have—for they are all that we have.

But the witness of scripture and the long tradition of Christian belief always should remind us that all we say and do in our weakness must be open to the direction of the Holy Spirit of God. When we remember our need always to be open to the Holy Spirit, then we can see why we who believe need the church—the one, holy, catholic, and apostolic church of all those joined to Christ as well as our particular community of faith, whether it be the Episcopal Church or some other. By myself I can so easily go astray, and I can so easily turn my belief in God into idolatry of myself, another person, or even a political agenda. Each of us needs continuity with that community of belief in which other human beings in the past have wrestled with the Spirit, trying to hear and respond to God in Jesus Christ—what we mean when we say that we are a church in apostolic succession. And we also need that community in which we now pray, that we may discern the Spirit.

The witness of the Bible, the doctrinal tradition of councils and creeds, the discipline of prayer, worship, and action, and our communion with one another and with God—all of these are essential components of how the church is the sacrament of God's presence. They are our heritage in the catholic faith mediated to us and brought to life in the particular historical conditions of our church community. By the grace of God, we believe, the Word of

Truth will be present with us in the process of our hearing and speaking.

The point is this: we who are Anglicans seek to live, as honestly as we can, in a twofold relationship with the Episcopal Church. On the one hand, we know it as an institution that is often divided and indecisive, willing to live with ambiguity and tension. In this clash and confusion of many voices, the Episcopal Church reflects our personal, human condition. We all, individually, try to determine in the complexity of our daily lives what it means to believe in God and what the consequences of that belief may be. In the church reaching a conclusion about complex social and theological issues is often a political process, one of trying to accommodate different points of view and human concerns; it can be messy, and sometimes the results are inconclusive and not pleasing to everyone. And yet, the struggle to reach a compromise or consensus remains an integral dimension of the church's life, just as it was in the time of the early councils of the church, as we try to discern the guidance of the Holy Spirit.

On the other hand, we believe that we are carrying out this very human and political process in continuity with the witness and teaching of Holy Scripture and the tradition of belief that comes to us in the one, holy, catholic, and apostolic church. The struggle—both political and theological—is how to weigh one against the other, and how to interpret the authority of both. But the process itself says who we are as Episcopalians: we *are* the church as we struggle; we are *being* the church, indeed we are believing *with* the church, in the process of seeking God's will for us. Consequently, we can say that in the very process of our struggle to believe *with* the church we also must say, as we do in the creeds, that we believe *in* the church; we believe it to be the community of faith in which God is present and in which God is guiding us to a deeper understanding of what we believe and ought to do. The church, we say, is the people of God and the body of Christ, a sign of God's purpose for the whole creation, the New Jerusalem and the temple of God.

This way of believing has shaped and characterized much of the history of Anglicanism. It is not for everyone; there are those who seek a greater certainty, and there are those who find its traditions too constrictive and authoritarian. But some have found in Anglicanism a way of believing in God that makes sense because it opens the way for transformation and salvation in Christ. As Michael Ramsey reminded us earlier, the Anglican Church "is sent not to commend itself as 'the best type of Christianity,' but by its very brokenness to point to the universal church wherein all have died." And, I would add, to serve as a sign of the hope of our calling in Christ.

I would not want to say that only because of the Episcopal Church did I come to believe in the God made known in Jesus Christ by the power of the Spirit. To say that would be idolatry of an institution, and it would certainly place much too heavy a burden on such a fragile community as the Episcopal Church! I would, however, want to say that the sacramental life in the Incarnation which the Episcopal Church has made possible for me has led me to believe as I do and has made it possible for me to believe with the community of the church. It has done so by providing me with a human space in which I can live with the tension of believing in God and believing that God is known in the ambiguity of human existence.

Receiving God's Word in heart and mind means receiving it in our lives and in the life of the community of which we are a part, and this community includes many other people. It includes those with whom we live and work everyday, those with whom we gather to worship, and those with whom we share a common humanity—all those people for whom we pray and who share life with us, Christian and non-Christian, religious and non-religious, "all sorts and conditions" of people, as the prayer book says. In other words, we receive God's Word to us and respond to it in and through the people of the world in which we live. God speaks to us in all of the ambiguities, sins, and failures of our lives as Christian people, but that Word of God to us is also spoken in the lives of all those other people whom God has made and with whom we are called to share in the life of God.

To believe that God's Word is spoken not just to us who believe, but to all those who live in the world and who share in God's world with us is the essence of an incarnational theology. It means that we who hear God's Word in scripture and in the tradition of belief in the church must always be ready to hear the Word that God speaks to us in our neighbors, in those who may not yet know the God who speaks.

This is the issue with which Anglican theologians, pastors, and lay people have struggled since the last century: Can God's Word be spoken to us in the words of those who do not yet know the God who speaks to them? Can God's Word come from radical critics of the Bible or from an "enemy" of the Christian faith? Can God's Word come from scientists, atheists, secularists, and humanists? Can it come from those who are condemned by the church as sinners or outsiders?[1]

In other words, a theology of the Incarnation is not an abstract, theological "game" in which some rather odd people like to engage while others ignore them. The Incarnation affects how Christian people regard God's world and their neighbors; it requires us to attend to God's presence in every human situation and in every voice, no matter how threatening. The Word of God can come to us in our greatest trials and temptations, as well as in joy and peace. It can come in the most unlikely of circumstances—remember that the risen Christ spoke to Paul when Paul was busy persecuting the church. And the Word of God can come to us in the ambiguities and dilemmas with which all human beings must live.

Believing in an Incarnate God and in God's redemptive work is not always easy. Making decisions about hard problems is not cut and dried, for there are no easy answers to the complex problems of human sexuality, death and life, social and economic justice, or the host of other questions with which we have to deal. All of these questions require listening, discerning, and responding out of our belief that the Holy and Incarnate God is present with us and that the Spirit of Christ can speak, even in strange voices. Listening requires much courage in those of us who believe, as we try to discern God's Word and interpret the tradition of Christian belief in the face of new and changing circumstances that shake the old foundations of Christian belief. Yes, of course, we still confess our belief in the God of Jesus Christ, but how can we now speak of that God? The images of God given to us in the ancient texts of the Bible are far different from the images of the cosmic God of interstellar space. Though they refer to the same God, how can new images be justified and explained to others?

Can belief in the basic doctrines and moral teachings of Christian faith find a place in an understanding of the world and of ourselves that seems increasingly alien to the understanding given to us in the Bible?

One way to deal with such questions, of course, is to deny the problem: to assert as a matter of faith that the biblical account of God, the world, and humankind is unchanging and must be accepted literally and without question. But that has not been the way of Anglicanism, at least not at what I believe to be its best. We Anglicans have striven to say that God's truth is richer and deeper than we can imagine, and certainly deeper and richer than we can express in any legal and moral code, language, or image. This is what our belief in the Incarnate Christ ought to teach us: that Jesus Christ calls us into relationship with a God "who surpasses all human understanding" and who is also Emmanuel, God with us. As a consequence, we can believe that we are always in the process of being led into new aspects of the truth of God made known to us in Christ, and that we must be ready to hear and to respond.

The process of experiencing and understanding change, of discerning new truths and rediscovering old ones, of waiting for God's Spirit to guide and direct us, always brings conflict and tension. But to be a community, as the Episcopal Church hopes to be, that has its center in the Incarnation of God in Christ means that we can find our unity as a church only from our unity in Christ—not from a book or from laws and structures, and not from what we like to call "the modern mind." Consequently, in all of the conflicts, tensions, and ambiguities which the church and individual Christians now know, Anglicanism, I believe, must continue to be a "middle way" which is always "on the way," looking, as the letter to the Hebrews puts it, to Jesus, "the pioneer and perfecter of our faith, who for the sake of the joy that was set before him endured the cross, disregarding its shame, and has taken his seat at the right hand of the throne of God" (Hebrews 12:1-2).

Endnotes

~ Chapter 1

1. For a history of this period, see David Holmes, *A Brief History of the Episcopal Church* (Valley Forge, Penn.: Trinity Press International, 1993).

~ Chapter 2

1. For a study of the context and authority of the Thirty-Nine Articles, see Henry Chadwick, "Tradition, Fathers, and Councils," in Stephen Sykes and John Booty, eds., *The Study of Anglicanism* (Minneapolis: Fortress Press, 1988). The Articles can be found in the *Book of Common Prayer* under "Historical Documents."

2. From *To Believe is to Pray: Readings from Michael Ramsey*, ed. James E. Griffiss (Cambridge, Mass.: Cowley Publications, 1996), 44-45.

3. Holmes, *A Brief History*, 31-37. For a full treatment of the colonial period, see John Woolverton, *Colonial Anglicanism in North America* (Detroit: Wayne State University Press, 1984).

4. Robert Bruce Mullin, *Episcopal Vision/American Reality* (New Haven: Yale University Press, 1986), 16.

5. Mullin, *Episcopal Vision*, 17-18.

∼ **Chapter 3**

1. The missionaries representing the Evangelical side of the Episcopal Church more often went overseas, especially to China.

2. See Holmes, *A Brief History*, 64.

3. See Holmes, *A Brief History*, especially for the limitations of Episcopal missionary work in the west, 65-70.

4. John Booty, *The Church in History* (New York: Seabury, 1979), 131.

5. In his various writings, Edward Pusey, the leader of the Oxford Movement, drew particularly on the sacramental theology of Cyril of Alexandria, for example.

6. Such a way of speaking of the Incarnation was common among theologians of the patristic period. In the early development of Anglican theology it was of great importance in Richard Hooker, to whom I have already referred. See his *Laws of Ecclesiastical Piety*, Book V.56.2, 20 and *passim*. It ought to be noted, however, that the nineteenth-century Tractarians would not have been quite so specific about "daughters"; as men of their times they would have believed that women derived their status through males.

7. The reference is to an important, but now neglected book by R. I. Wilberforce, *The Doctrine of the Incarnation of Our Lord Jesus Christ in its Relation to Mankind and to the Church*, published in London in 1848. See also Pusey's "The Holy Eucharist a Comfort to the Penitent," a sermon preached before the University of Oxford, Easter 4, 1843. In an appendix he traces this theme in the writings of other Anglican divines, especially Lancelot Andrewes, Jeremy Taylor, John Donne, William Laud, and George Herbert.

∼ **Chapter 4**

1. Report of the Anglo-Catholic Congress of 1923. Such congresses were held frequently during the early part of this century, though unfortunately the reports are only to be found in highly specialized libraries.

2. From *The Doctrine of Sacrifice* (London: Macmillan, 1853), xli. The citation is from William J. Wolf, ed., *The Spirit of Anglicanism* (Wilton, Conn.: Morehouse-Barlow, 1979). Wolf's essay is an excellent introduction to the theology of Maurice.

3. Booty, *The Church in History*, 139.

4. Bernard Markwell, *The Anglican Left: Radical Social Reformers in the Church of England and the Protestant Episcopal Church, 1846-1954* (Brooklyn: Carlson Publishing, 1991), 144. See also John Orens, "Politics and the Kingdom: The Legacy of the Anglican Left" in Paul Elmen, ed., *The Anglican Moral Choice* (Wilton, Conn.: Morehouse-Barlow, 1983); and Pamela W. Darling, *New Wine: The Story of Women Transforming Leadership and Power in the Episcopal Church* (Cambridge, Mass.: Cowley Publications, 1994).

5. From *On Journey* (New York: Dutton, 1937), 163; quoted in Markwell, *The Anglican Left*, 191. Markwell comments, "It is clear that for Vida Scudder socialism is the handmaiden of Christianity." And later, "Vida Scudder never lost the Mauricean passion for unity—ultimately religious and social problems were one to her—and as she became more religious she also became more radical" (204). Fabian socialism, it should be noted, differed from Marxism in that it was evolutionary rather than deterministic.

6. Markwell, *The Anglican Left*, 218.

7. *Ibid.*, 222.

8. William Stringfellow, *My People Is the Enemy* (New York: Holt, Rinehart and Winston, 1964), 97. All of Stringfellow's books are now out of print, but a comprehensive selection of his writings can be found in Bill Wylie Kellerman's *A Keeper of the Word: Selected Writings of William Stringfellow* (Grand Rapids: Eerdmans, 1994).

9. William Stringfellow, *A Private and Public Faith* (Grand Rapids: Eerdmans, 1962), 40-41.

10. William Stringfellow, *Dissenter in a Great Society* (New York: Holt, Rinehart and Winston, 1966), 163-164.

11. The full text of the Quadrilateral can be found in the *Book of Common Prayer* (1979) in the section "Historical Documents."

12. For a fuller discussion, see my *Church, Ministry, and Unity: A Divine Commission* (Oxford: Basil Blackwell, 1983).

13. The revised text can be found in J. Robert Wright, ed., *A Communion of Communions: One Eucharistic Fellowship* (New York: Seabury Press, 1979), 16–17.

14. For a fuller discussion of all these themes, see William L. Sachs, *The Transformation of Anglicanism: From State Church to Global Communion* (Cambridge: Cambridge University Press, 1993).

～ Chapter 5

1. The phrase "and the Son" (*filioque* in Latin) was not part of the original creed. It was added by the western church during later controversies about Arianism, and it is rejected by the Orthodox churches of the East, for reasons both theological and historical. It is still a source of contention between the two great branches of the Christian church. There is some movement in the churches of the Anglican Communion to remove it from the prayer book version of the creed, or at least to put it in brackets, in order that the creed may be more genuinely ecumenical. However, there are major theological problems about doing so, since the phrase and the theological doctrine it represents have been a part of western theology and spirituality for many centuries.

～ Chapter 7

1. A. M. Ramsey, *The Gospel and the Catholic Church* (Cambridge, Mass.: Cowley Publications, 1990), 220.

2. Frederick Borsch, "All Things Necessary to Salvation," in Frederick Borsch, ed., *Anglicanism and the Bible* (Wilton, Conn.: Morehouse-Barlow, 1984), 225.

3. John Macquarrie, *Principles of Christian Theology,* Preface to first edition (New York: Charles Scribner's Sons, 1966). There was a second edition in 1977.

4. The Athanasian Creed was for long mistakenly attributed to the fourth-century theologian Athanasius, who opposed the

Arian heresy. It is sometimes used in the Church of England, but not in the Episcopal Church. The text is found in the *Book of Common Prayer,* "Historical Documents," 864.

5. Leonel L. Mitchell, *Praying Shapes Believing: A Theological Commentary on the Book of Common Prayer* (Harrisburg: Morehouse Publishing, 1985), 2.

6. Louis Weil, "The Gospel in Anglicanism," in Sykes and Booty, *The Study of Anglicanism,* 55.

7. *The Hymnal 1982,* #302. The text is dated as CE 110.

～ Chapter 8

1. There have been two recent examples of studies by Anglicans that seek to explore such questions from the perspective of the Incarnation: Arthur Peacocke, *Theology for a Scientific Age: Being and Becoming—Natural, Divine, and Human* (Minneapolis: Fortress Press, 1993); and Charles Hefling, ed., *Our Selves, Our Souls and Bodies: Sexuality and the Household of God* (Cambridge, Mass.: Cowley Publications, 1996).

Resources

~ **Episcopal Church History**

Two histories of the Episcopal Church have been published recently and both are well worth reading: Robert Prichard's *A History of the Episcopal Church* (Morehouse, 1991) and David Holmes' *A Brief History of the Episcopal Church* (Trinity, 1993). Professor Holmes' history is particularly well-written and has excellent photographs. Don Armentrout's and Robert Slocum's *Documents of Witness* (Church Hymnal, 1994) brings together readings from primary sources in the history of the Episcopal Church from 1782-1985.

Good scholarly studies of the history of the Episcopal Church are also available. John Woolverton's *Colonial Anglicanism in North America* (Wayne State University, 1984) is a thorough account of the colonial churches in America. Diana Hochstedt Butler's *Standing Against the Whirlwind* (Oxford, 1995) studies the Evangelical party in the Episcopal Church and its effect on the piety, identity, theology, and mission of the church, while Robert Bruce Mullin's *Episcopal Vision/American Reality* (Yale, 1986) examines the high church vision as exemplified in the figure of John Henry Hobart, bishop of New York. A book by Allen C. Guelzo, *For the Union of Evangelical Christendom* (Pennsylvania State, 1994), also explores Evangelicalism through the history of the Reformed Episcopal Church. All four books are excellent examples of the good and accessible historical scholarship available from university presses.

For the history of women in the Episcopal Church, Catherine Prelinger's *Episcopal Women: Gender, Spirituality, and Commitment in an American Mainline Denomination* (Oxford, 1992) is an excellent resource, bringing together essays by women scholars in religious history and sociology. Mary Sudman Donovan's *A Different Call* (Morehouse, 1986), looks at lay women's ministries in the church between 1850-1920, while Pamela W. Darling's *New Wine* (Cowley, 1994) examines the history of the leadership and ordination of women in the Episcopal Church and the consecration of the first woman bishop.

～ Anglicanism

For a good overview of the history and theology of Anglicanism, see Stephen Sykes's and John Booty's *The Study of Anglicanism* (SPCK/Fortress, 1988), which brings together thirty-one short essays on all aspects of Anglicanism by scholars from America, England, Ireland, and Canada. Each essay begins with a short bibliography of relevant works in the field, so it is an indispensable reference tool for the student of Anglicanism.

Another valuable reference work is G. R. Evans's and J. Robert Wright's *The Anglican Tradition* (SPCK/Fortress, 1991), which contains documents and texts from every period of Anglican history throughout the Anglican Communion, beginning with the early church and ending with the ecumenical movement. Urban T. Holmes's *What is Anglicanism?* (Morehouse, 1982) provides a brief introduction to Anglicanism, including the Anglican approach to the Bible, liturgy, episcopacy, pastoral care, and mission.

Two short books from Forward Movement Publications sketch the theology of Anglicanism and important figures from Anglican history such as Jeremy Taylor and F. D. Maurice: David L. Edwards, *What Anglicans Believe* (rev. 1996) and Lee W. Gibbs, *The Middle Way: Voices of Anglicanism* (1991). *The Spirit of Anglicanism,* edited by William J. Wolf (Morehouse, 1979), provides essays on Hooker, Maurice, and Temple. *The Spirit of the Oxford Movement: Tractarian Essays* by Owen Chadwick (Cambridge, 1995) gives an overview of the Oxford Movement and the high church tradition, as well as primary sources.

～ Anglican Social Witness and Mission

In addition to the works on Vida Scudder and William Stringfellow cited in the notes, there are several good books on the Anglican social witness. Robert Hood's *Social Teachings in the Episcopal Church* (Morehouse, 1990) provides an overview of Anglicanism's social theology and witness in the areas of war and peace, race, family life and sexuality, and economics. Fredrica Harris Thompsett's *Courageous Incarnation* (Cowley, 1993) explores the implications of the doctrine of the Incarnation for the church today in the areas of childhood, work, sexuality, and aging.

Alister McGrath's *The Renewal of Anglicanism* (Morehouse, 1993), traces the history and development of evangelism in the Anglican tradition, while Ian T. Douglas' new study of Anglican mission, *Fling Out the Banner! The National Church Ideal and the Foreign Mission of the Episcopal Church* (Church Hymnal, 1996), provides a history of foreign mission from the early nineteenth century to the present.

～ Anglican Theology and Worship

For an introduction to Anglican theology, see the essays in
Arthur Vogel, ed. *Theology in Anglicanism* (Morehouse-Barlow, 1984) and James E. Griffiss, ed., *Anglican Theology and
Pastoral Care* (Morehouse-Barlow, 1985). Geoffrey Wain-
wright's collection of essays to mark the centenary of the
publication of *Lux Mundi, Keeping the Faith* (Fortress, 1988),
provides a fine evaluation of the influence of *Lux Mundi* on
Anglican theology.

There are a number of excellent books on Anglican
worship available today. Two that focus particularly on an
Anglican theology of the eucharist are H. R. MacAdoo and
Kenneth W. Stephenson, *The Mystery of the Eucharist in the
Anglican Tradition: What Happens at Holy Communion?* (The
Canterbury Press, 1995) and Charles Miller, *Praying the
Eucharist* (Morehouse, 1995). J. Robert Wright's *Prayer
Book Spirituality* (Church Hymnal, 1989) is an interesting
and useful collection of devotional writings on prayer, the
church year, and the sacraments from classical Anglican
sources, including Richard Hooker, George Herbert, and
John Henry Hobart.

～ Audiovisual Resources

A wide variety of videotapes are available to supplement
any study of the history and theology of Anglicanism. The
Center for the Ministry of Teaching at Virginia Theological
Seminary (3737 Seminary Road, Alexandria, VA 22304)
has a library of audio and video resources available to
parishes.

Another excellent resource is provided by The Episcopal
Radio/TV Foundation, which has audiocassettes and videotapes for purchase or rental. Their Anglican section includes material by a wide variety of Anglicans, including
John Westerhoff, John Stott, Robert Runcie, and George

Carey. Videotapes that could be used in conjunction with this book include topics such as the Anglican tradition, the Apostles' Creed, the Oxford Movement, and the Episcopal Church's mission to the western frontier.

Questions for Group Study

This book may be used for an eight-session introductory study of Anglicanism, reading one chapter for each meeting. In order to enrich the discussion, questions should be read along with the chapter, before the class meets, as individual preparation for responding to the questions is sometimes required. The questions may be used in large or small groups, though you may find some are more fruitfully discussed in pairs or groups of three.

∼ Chapter 1

Those who grow up in the church are profoundly influenced by the community that first shaped their faith—the church of their parents and grandparents. It is the first inkling we get of what it means to be "religious" even if we go on to reject that experience in the course of becoming an adult.

1. What was your first impression of the Anglican Church? How has your image of the church changed as you have come to know it better?

2. The author describes his experience of growing up in a church in downtown Baltimore. Looking back from an adult perspective, how would you describe the church you grew up in—theologically, socially, economically? What do you remember best about the ministers, the building, the other people in the congregation?

2. In what ways do you think the churches of your childhood and adolescence still shape the way you think about God, and the ideas you have about what the church is and does? How do they affect your ideas of what it means to be an Anglican?

∼ Chapter 2

An important theme of the second chapter is a tension that lies at the very core of being an Anglican: trying to balance the need for a solid, continuing tradition and identity with the need for development, renewal, and change. As the author reminds us, this tension goes back to the time of Hooker and the Reformation, when Anglicans first had to define their identity in relationship to both the Roman Catholics and the Reformers. It reappeared in another form when the American colonies won their independence and Anglicans were no longer part of an established church. It is with us today as we try to discern God's will in the midst of conflicting opinions regarding questions of social ethics, the language of worship, and human sexuality.

1. Discuss several theological, liturgical, or pastoral questions that have been raised recently in your congregation that illustrate this tension between "We've always done it this way!" and "But this is what the church ought to be doing now!" What were the underlying issues? How did you deal with the conflict?

2. Anglicans have long been known for their use of three sources of authority for their knowledge of God: scripture, reason, and tradition. In what ways do you see this "three-legged stool" being used in the church today?

3. What do you think "tradition" means for your parish, as opposed to habit or custom? What sources of authority do you turn to when deciding how to handle change and continuity in your congregation and in the larger church? Does it help to know that this kind of tension is part of being Anglican?

∼ **Chapter 3**
In his third chapter the author describes several approaches to theology and faith found in Anglicanism, from the Evangelical witness of Wilberforce to the Anglo-Catholicism of Pusey and the Broad Church leanings of a preacher like Phillips Brooks. Each approach has a distinct value that has enriched the Anglican tradition, whether it be an emphasis on social outreach, personal discipline and prayer, education, reverence for liturgy, or love of knowledge.

1. Which of these three approaches—Evangelical, Anglo-Catholic, and Broad Church—best describes your own spirituality? Why? How did you learn of it? Are there elements of other approaches you would like to learn more about?

2. Which approach best describes the focus of your congregation? How does it show itself in the liturgy, programs, preaching, and outreach of your parish? Are other approaches present as well?

3. Do you see signs of a renewal taking place in the church today? If so, where? How do you think the church will be different in the twenty-first century?

～ Chapter 4

In the area of mission and outreach, Anglicans have held different and often conflicting points of view. Some believe that religion and politics should never mix, that church and society should be kept strictly separate, while others believe that the kingdom of God must be concerned with the material world as well as the spiritual. Some nineteenth-century Anglo-Catholic clergy, for example, avoided reading the newspaper or voting, but were known for their mission work in the slums; Evelyn Underhill was taught that visiting the poor was part of a balanced spiritual life, along with Bible reading and prayer; Vida Scudder became a socialist and worked for labor reform. Recently some Anglicans have been strongly influenced by Roman Catholic liberation theology and the need for solidarity with the indigent and marginal, while an equal number insist that evangelism and conversion of life is the most urgent priority.

1. What role do mission and outreach play in your own spirituality? What role do they play in your congregation? How and by whom was your congregation founded?

2. What differences do you see between social activism and a distinctively Christian social witness? Do the ideas of F. D. Maurice about Christian fellowship and solidarity presented in this chapter change or confirm the way you think about outreach?

3. Read through the various forms given for The Prayers of the People, beginning on page 383 of *The Book of Common Prayer*. What do prayer and outreach have in common? How does your corporate and personal prayer inform your outreach and mission?

∼ **Chapter 5**

This chapter explores the beliefs of Anglicans, for whom the doctrine of the Incarnation is especially important. We believe in a God who came to "dwell among us," as the prologue to John's gospel states, both as God and as a human being who suffered death on the cross, was raised from the dead, and continues to identify with the human condition, its sufferings and joys.

1. Richard Hooker wrote that because of the Incarnation, we can say "all things that are, are good.... Nature is nothing else but God's instrument." In what ways does Hooker's sense of the goodness of all creation inform your own spirituality? How does a belief in the goodness of creation show itself in your own parish and its attitude toward its building and property, its music, its festivals, its educational program, its fostering of the arts?

2. Read through the Nicene Creed (BCP 358), the Apostles' Creed (BCP 96), the Creed of St. Athanasius (BCP 864), and the Chaledonian Definition (BCP 864). What common themes strike you? In what ways do these early statements of belief reflect your own faith in God? How do they differ?

3. Can you imagine some ways that a strong belief in the Incarnation would affect your parish's stewardship, especially the money given for outreach?

∼ **Chapter 6**

In discussing Anglican prayer and worship, the author comments that the 1979 *Book of Common of Prayer* marks a change in our worship. For a very long time the service of Morning Prayer, with its emphasis on the Word, was normative in most parishes three out of four Sundays, whereas now the focus is on the eucharist, with a greater emphasis on congregational participation in the service of baptism as well.

1. What do you see as the primary emphasis in your congregation's worship? Would you say that your parish is more eucharistically centered, places more emphasis on preaching and Bible study, or is evenly balanced between the two? How does this emphasis shape your spirituality and beliefs?

2. When you were baptized, was the liturgy part of the main Sunday service or a private family event? How are baptisms celebrated in your congregation now? Do you think the recovery of baptism as a primary sacrament of identity for Anglican Christians is making a difference in the way Anglicans live out their faith? If so, how?

3. When have you been challenged to have the "courage to worship" in your life? Did the sense of being a part of a sacramental community strengthen your faith at that time? How has your worship in the church informed your belief in God?

∼ **Chapter 7**

This chapter focuses on the questions of Anglican identity and authority. Authority is a thorny issue for many Anglicans, since for us ultimate authority does not reside in a person, such as the pope, nor do we subscribe to a formal confession apart from the Apostles' and Nicene creeds. While many Anglicans are comfortable with ambiguity in matters of faith, others have criticized that Anglicans are "fuzzy" in their beliefs, unable to provide firm answers to questions of doctrine and church practice.

1. Why do you think people look for absolute certainties in their faith? What kinds of certainties do you think people are looking for? What questions of faith do you seek answers to?

2. Archbishop Michael Ramsey once said that we have not been given the Anglican faith as the "best" kind of Christianity, but its very brokenness is a sign of the universal church, still waiting for redemption. Do you find this remark helpful in thinking about the frustrations and shortcomings of your own church, and the imperfections of its members? Or does it sound as if he were making excuses for the church?

3. Read again the second-century hymn quoted at the end of this chapter. Is this a prayer you could pray for the church today? Do you share the author's belief in the church "as a community which, with all of its diversity and brokenness, is called beyond itself into God"? How might the current debates in the church be changed with this understanding of the church in mind?

∼ **Chapter 8**
In this chapter the author discusses the church itself as a sacrament, allowing us to believe *with* the church even when we have difficulty believing *in* the church. He also

reminds us that prayer is a sacrament: in prayer, as in the eucharist, we offer ourselves, our souls and bodies, to God.

1. Which sacraments of the church have been the most meaningful for you? Why? How have they been means of grace for you? Are there other sacraments you would like to participate in, given the opportunity?

2. How would you answer the author's question, "Can God's Word be spoken to us in the words of those who do not yet know the God who speaks to them?" When have you most often heard God's Word through the words or actions of those outside the church?

3. Prayer can take many forms in a congregation, including silent prayer, intercession, sacraments, prayers for healing, centering prayer, praise and worship, meditation, retreats, saying the daily office, and following the Stations of the Cross. What are the different ways that your church shows itself to be a "place of prayer"? What kinds of praying seem to be the main focus—or the most valued—in your church? What forms of prayer do you find the most meaningful? The most difficult?

Cowley Publications is a ministry of the Society of St. John the Evangelist, a religious community for men in the Episcopal Church. Emerging from the Society's tradition of prayer, theological reflection, and diversity of mission, the press is centered in the rich heritage of the Anglican Communion.

Cowley Publications seeks to provide books, audio cassettes, and other resources for the ongoing theological exploration and spiritual development of the Episcopal Church and others in the body of Christ. To this end, it is dedicated to developing a new generation of theological writers, encouraging them to produce timely, creative, and stimulating publications of excellence, and making these publications available widely, reaching both clergy and lay persons.